DECENTRALIZATION, LOCAL GOVERNANCE, AND LOCAL ECONOMIC DEVELOPMENT IN MONGOLIA

AUGUST 2021

ASIAN DEVELOPMENT BANK

ADB

CONTENTS

TABLES, FIGURES, AND BOXES

BOXES

ACKNOWLEDGMENTS

This publication was prepared by the Public Management, Financial Sector and Regional Cooperation and Integration Division (EAPF) of the East Asia Department, in close cooperation with The Asia Foundation (Mongolia Chapter). The preparation of the publication was financed by the Governance Thematic Group in the Sustainable Development and Climate Change Department, under TA 9387-REG: Strengthening Institutions for Localizing Agenda 2030 for Sustainable Development. The publication was finalized for publication by Hans van Rijn (EAPF); initial drafting was done by Roger Shotton (Local Development Associates). The authors like to especially thank Mark Koenig, Country Representative of The Asia Foundation in Mongolia, for his contributions as peer reviewer. The publication benefited greatly from the numerous consultations with both central and local government officials, civil society organizations, and development partners in Mongolia.

ABBREVIATIONS

DLA	Directorate of Local Administration
EMP	environmental management plan
LATUG	Law on Administrative and Territorial Units and Their Governance
LDF	Local Development Fund
LLA	local-level agreement
MALA	Mongolian Association of Local Authorities
MNAO	Mongolian National Audit Office
MNT	Mongolian togrog
MOF	Ministry of Finance
NAOG	National Academy of Governance
NDA	National Development Agency
NGO	nongovernment organization
PBG	performance-based grant
PFM	public financial management
SDC	Swiss Agency for Development and Cooperation
SLP3	Sustainable Livelihoods Project – Phase 3
SNG	subnational government
UNDP	United Nations Development Programme

GLOSSARY

aimag	province (first tier of subnational government)
bagh	rural ward
dzud	periodic weather sequence of severe drought and extreme cold affecting livestock and rural livelihoods
ger	portable, sturdy tent
hural	elected assembly
khoroo	urban ward
soum	district (second tier of subnational government)
State *hural*	National Parliament

SYNOPSIS

Introduction

This publication discusses the formal features of Mongolia's decentralized governance system and the extent to which these features translate into the working environment of subnational governments (SNGs). The publication takes the perspective of two of the roles typically assigned to SNGs: (i) the provision of public services and (ii) the promotion of local economic development.

In doing so, the publication assesses the opportunities and constraints posed by the current political, legal, fiscal, human resource, and administrative environment in which SNGs operate and recommends how to strengthen their role. This synopsis presents an overview of the issues discussed in detail in the remainder of the publication.

The publication was prepared before the coronavirus disease (COVID-19) pandemic reached Mongolia and does not assess the impact the pandemic has had on local economic development and service delivery at the subnational level. Globally, the pandemic has highlighted the critical role of local governments as frontline providers of public services, which reinforces the recommendations regarding the need to strengthen the enabling environment for SNGs in Mongolia.

Constraints Facing Subnational Governments in the Implementation of Their Responsibilities

SNGs in Mongolia have an important role in local service delivery and local development, but this potential is undermined by several constraints. It is common to refer to "local capacity problems," but that can be a misleading diagnosis, suggesting a need to focus on training. There are indeed problems in current human resource capacity building arrangements, but there are deeper problems:

(i)   The policy, legal, and regulatory framework is sometimes unclear or inconsistent and usually is not translated into clear operational guidance for SNG personnel, such that even if more resources were devoted to training, the content is often missing.

(ii)   The local institutional setup duplicates some functions and blurs accountabilities, gives too small a role to elected *hurals* (elected assembly), and promotes a vicious cycle that undermines their potential representative and developmental role. It prevents either the *hurals* or the governors from supervising local deconcentrated staff.

(iii)   Financing and budgeting arrangements, despite the reforms of the new Budget Law constitute a straitjacket, precluding local discretion that is the rationale for decentralization. This undercuts the scope for input, supervision, or coordination over local sector departments by local authorities, and in other cases, allows undue discretion and untransparent behavior (e.g., in *aimag* [province] budgetary allocations to *soums* [districts]).

These constraints compromise the ability of SNGs to fulfill their potential. In particular, basic local service delivery spending is:

(i)   less effective than it could be in meeting often highly local needs and priorities because many responsibilities are still under central government control. Even for those SNGs formally decentralized, they are subject to a centralized and rigid budget decision-making process, with little guidance on translating policy into spending;

(ii)   less equitable across SNG areas than it could be because of the significant variance in resources per capita allocated between *soums* and *aimags*;

(iii) less efficient than it could be in translating resources into service outputs because of the rigidities noted above, the weak guidance and incentives surrounding the budget process, and the problems in treasury and procurement; and

(iv)   less accountable than it could be because of the lack of clarity and overlaps in local institutional oversight roles.

Meanwhile, the promotion of broader local development through regulatory and convening powers is:

(i)   often limited due to the relatively weak powers of this sort assigned to SNGs;

(ii)   compromised by the laws or regulations underlying these powers that are not always consistent or appropriate (e.g., as in the land-use framework);

(iii) further compromised by the frequent lack of clear guidance on their operational application (e.g., as for the mining environmental management plans or local-level agreements); and

(iv)   less accountable than it could be because of the lack of clarity and overlaps in local institutional oversight roles.

Recommendations

1. Strengthen the Policy, Legal, and Regulatory Framework

The 2016 Government Resolution on decentralization policy and the recently formed State *hural* working group provided an important opportunity to develop a clearer and more consistent national framework for subnational governance and service delivery. This could include establishment of an interministerial working group chaired by the Cabinet Secretariat to develop an action plan to implement the directions set out in the Government Resolution, and which would map the implications for the sector ministries concerned to address issues such as

(i)   the scope for making legal provisions to recognize the specific challenges faced by urban SNGs and to mandate them with the responsibilities and powers needed;

(ii)   the implications, opportunities, and challenges regarding the role, operation, and performance of SNGs in light of recent key pieces of legislation (e.g., the Development Policy and Planning Law and the recently revised Civil Service Law);

(iii) for SNG expenditure responsibilities, the implications of the functional assignment policy and how to implement it, which functions are to be transferred and when, the nature of the desired form of decentralization (devolution or delegation), and the budget expenditure implications for SNGs;

(iv) for SNG revenues and transfers, the adequacy and equity of current arrangements in view of increased future SNG spending responsibilities; the scope for increasing revenue powers (sources and rate decision powers) of SNGs; and scope for revising transfer mechanisms to allow greater transparency, equity, and SNG discretion as might be achieved, for example, through introducing simple formula-based conditional grants to finance the decentralized subsector responsibilities agreed upon; and

(v) for SNG budgeting, ensuring that the Medium-Term Fiscal Framework budget ceilings for base expenditures communicated to *aimags* in the Budget Circular are respected in the budget proposals submitted to the central government; and that *aimags* communicate budget ceilings to their *soums* to improve discipline priority setting, and to encourage budget cutback choices to be made locally rather than centrally. It would also be important to provide similar advance budget ceilings to *aimags* and *soums* for delegated social expenditures.

The Local Development Fund (LDF) appears to need review and clarification of several policy issues: (i) the nature of the eligible spending menus at *aimag* and *soum* levels and how they relate to future SNG sector capital spending; (ii) the rationale for sharing mining royalty revenues by origin into LDF accounts in view of the major inequities arising; and (iii) the rationale for the General Local Development Fund formula itself that penalizes more highly populated SNGs, and includes other inconsistencies and anomalies.

As to the central monitoring of SNGs, the corollary of any move to greater decentralization is that the central government can track and analyze SNG revenues and spending. This would require more comprehensive and analytically useful reporting by *aimags* to the Ministry of Finance, including similar reporting on the *soums* (currently missing altogether); and a focal unit for SNG finance within the Ministry of Finance where all reports on transfers to SNGs and SNG own-revenues and sectoral expenditures arrive. At the same time, some thought should be given to the appropriate forms of external audit and supervision by the Mongolian National Audit Office and State Inspection Agency to ensure that resources are used to provide more regular and consistent audits than at present.

Regarding performance incentives, there are opportunities to review the scope for developing monitoring and incentive mechanisms for SNGs tied to fiscal transfers, building on those already practiced, such as the performance-based grant or annual performance assessment mechanism being tested alongside the Local Development Fund under the Sustainable Livelihoods Project Phase 3, but for which a more sustainable mechanism urgently needs to be developed.

While discussion of SNG functions tends to be equated with narrower spending responsibilities, the broader set of regulatory powers enjoyed by SNGs deserves review since these are critical to several pressing issues related to urban governance, local economic development, and regulation of extractive industries. This review would focus on the adequacy of current powers and on possible unclear or inconsistent regulations arising in the exercise of these powers.

Any future policy consultation and development on SNGs must include other voices to represent the views of SNG governors and *hurals*, possibly through the Mongolian Association of Local Authorities, and those of civil society organizations and nongovernment organizations (NGOs) working with SNGs. It would be useful to organize a forum where stakeholders could periodically meet central government authorities and State *hural* members on policy around subnational governance.

2. Further Develop the Capacities of Subnational Governments

There is a need for institutionalizing a mechanism to ensure regular induction, refresher training, and ad hoc support to SNG personnel for their specific duties and for policy and legislation related to these duties along with guidance on day-to-day handling of duties. Following the guidelines recommended in this publication, this could be a mix of both core, supply-driven capacity support and more ad hoc, flexible, context-specific, demand-driven support. There are important lessons from several ongoing projects as to what works well.

Practical guidelines and related case materials are needed to implement or comply with national policies, laws, and regulations, whether related to local planning, budgeting, service delivery, regulating the environment or local economic development to help SNG personnel, officials, and *hural* members learn what to do. Some materials have been developed in some areas under specific projects, but these are generic. The institutional capacity to produce, revise, and update guidance materials as needed should be created, possibly within the National Academy of Governance or a similar training agency.

3. Promote Local Accountability and Transparency

Reforms are needed for financing mechanisms and budget norms to allow greater local discretion. A lack of discretionary decision-making power is perhaps the major impediment to any substantial degree of citizen and NGO engagement with the SNGs.

Consider building on the Sustainable Livelihoods Project Phase 3 performance-based grant and annual performance assessment mechanisms, and link simple incentives with fiscal transfer arrangements to reward SNGs that make efforts in this area.

Provision of operational guidance must be provided to SNGs on how to implement the numerous legal provisions that exist to mandate disclosure and engagement by SNGs (e.g., for participatory planning, procurement, or monitoring service delivery). Such guidance would need to feed into the institutionalized training programs indicated above.

Finally, support and training for CSOs and the media to encourage informed, investigative coverage of SNG affairs is necessary.

SUBNATIONAL GOVERNANCE IN MONGOLIA

INSTITUTIONAL AND POLICY CONTEXT

This section outlines the institutional arrangements and status of policy for subnational governance in Mongolia.

A. Institutional Structures

1. Subnational Government Institutions

■ General Setup

Mongolia is a unitary state. The subnational government (SNG) is established under Chapter IV of the Constitution and under the Law on Administrative and Territorial Units and their Governance (2006), hereafter referred to as LATUG. It is aligned as a tiered structure (Table 1 and Figure 1).

The two levels of the institutional setup each follow a dual structure seen in other post-socialist states:

Table 1: Structure of Mongolia's Subnational Governments

Capital City	Other Areas
Ulaanbaatar	21 *Aimags*
9 Districts	330 *Soums*
151 *Khoroos*	1,559 *Baghs*

Note: *aimag* = province, *soum* = subdistrict, whether urban or rural; *khoroo* = urban ward; *bagh* = rural ward.

Source: Asian Development Bank (compiled from the Law on Administrative and Territorial Units and Their Governance 2006).

(i) A legislative assembly (*hural*), supported by a full-time secretary, and (at *aimag* level) other supporting staff under the secretary. *Hurals* serve a four-year term.

(ii) An executive branch headed by a governor and a deputy governor. These officials are indirectly elected and serve for the same four-year term as the *hurals*. A list of candidates is nominated by the *hural* at that level and from that list a selection is made by the prime minister for *aimag* governors and by the *aimag* governor for *soum* governors. The governor and deputy governor oversee the two executive arms of the SNG and (a) directly supervise the Governor's Office and its departments and staff; and (b) provide administrative oversight of deconcentrated subnational sector ministry departments, their facilities (schools, clinics, etc.), and staff, but who are under the primary supervision of their central ministries or other central agencies.

This dual structure is usually justified by the separation of policymaking and oversight (the local legislature) from execution (the local executive) and aims to provide institutionalized checks and balances. Because of this dual structure, the SNG paradigm in Mongolia does not fit well with the notion of local government insofar as the local government carries connotations of a single, unified corporate entity with a clearly defined political and policy mandate. Failure to recognize this can lead to serious misunderstanding.

The *baghs* (rural wards), like the *khoroos* (urban wards) in Ulaanbaatar, are not strictly an institutional tier of the SNG organizational structure insofar as there are no elected *bagh hurals*, and no officials serve at the *bagh* level per se. However, some (like teachers or health staff) may be deployed in *baghs* from their *soum* line departments. The *baghs* serve as administrative areas and as a locus for mandatory consultation and collective action. The LATUG provides for periodic *bagh* assemblies where residents can come together for consultations and to formulate priorities and needs, which are relayed to the *soum* governors and *hurals*. They also elect *bagh* governors to serve as community leaders.

Figure 1: Schematic View of Subnational Government in Mongolia (Outside Ulaanbaatar)

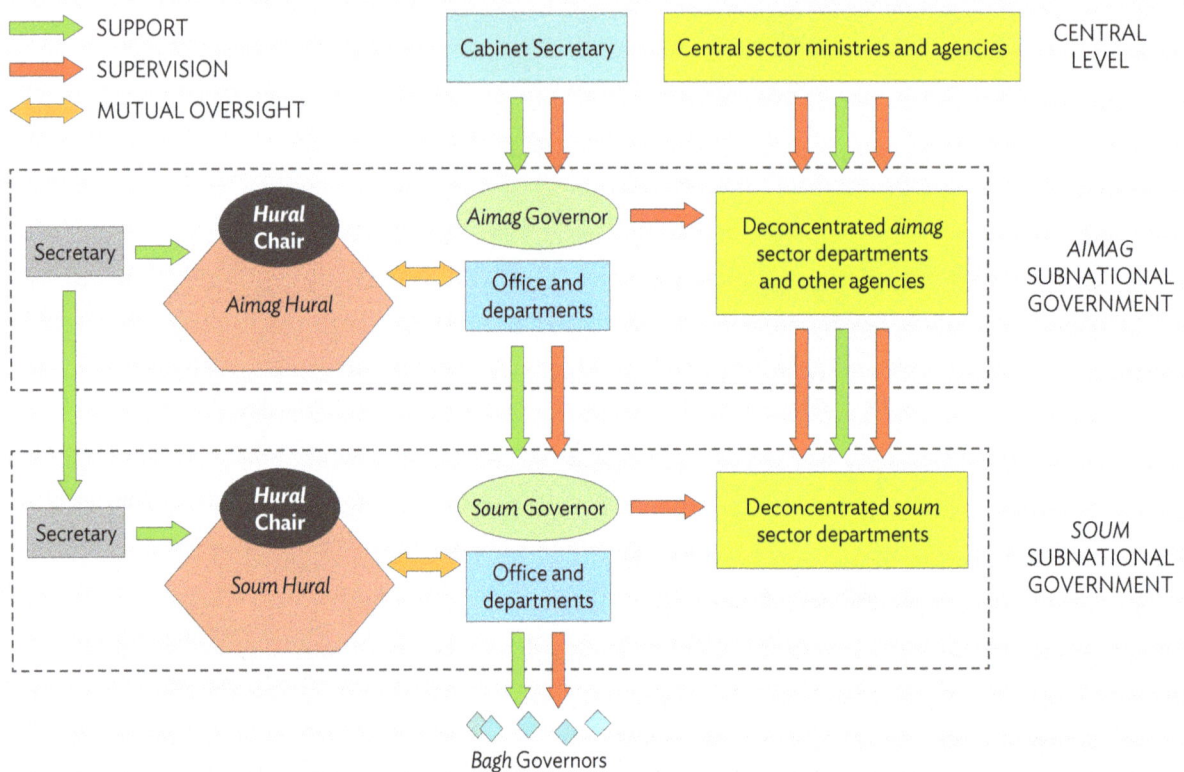

Source: Asian Development Bank (compiled by the authors).

Roles and Powers

In principle, the Governor's Office is responsible for planning, implementation, and reporting on the delivery of local public services, while the *hural* is responsible for setting local policy and priorities and for monitoring and oversight of planning and implementation. The LATUG sets out the respective roles and powers of *aimag* and *soum hurals* as indicated in Box 1.

Articles 8 and 12 in the Law on State Supervision and Inspection (2003, revised 2010) also mandate SNG governors and *hurals* to oversee each other.

Box 1: **Roles and Powers**

Hurals (under Articles 18 and 19)

- Approval and amendment of socioeconomic strategy, governor's budget, or budget implementation
- Approval, review, and evaluation of governor's activities
- Monitoring and evaluation of governor's implementation of *hural* resolutions or legislation
- Establishment and oversight of local development fund with nonbudgetary revenues
- Coordination of local socioeconomic development strategy with regional strategy
- Imposition of fees and tariffs within limits of legislation
- Approval of land-use management plans and programs
- Exercise of local property ownership rights (*hurals* are the legal property owners of local socioeconomic infrastructure such as wells, kindergartens, schools, clinics, hospitals, parks, and playgrounds).

Subnational Government Governors (under Article 29)

- Preparation of plans and budgets for submission to *hural* for review and approval, and organization of implementation for approved plans and budgets
- Development of projects and programs to implement plans and budgets
- Preparation of implementation reports
- Implementation of state policies and laws, and of local *hural* laws and resolutions
- Development of agriculture, land, and natural resources consistent with state policy and laws, and with *hural* decisions and laws
- Development of local infrastructure
- Administration of social services consistent with state policy and law and with *hural* decisions

Promulgation of policies and laws on law and order and security passed by central government and by the local *hural*, which ensures their application

hural = elected assembly.

Source: Law on Administrative and Territorial Units and Their Governance (2006).

The LATUG also mandates *aimag* governors and staff to supervise and support *soum* governors, as part of the vertical chain below the Cabinet Secretariat.

■ The Dual Institutions of Subnational Governance: A Closer Look

Governors

The executive branch is headed by the governor and deputy governor. Governors are indirectly elected. A list of candidates is nominated by the *hural* at that level, from which the prime minister selects governors for *aimags*, and the *aimag* governor selects governors for *soums*.[1] They serve a 4-year term.

The governor is supported by the head of the Governor's Office, which has departments or units for finance, public administration, monitoring, and public relations.

---

[1]   In Ulaanbaatar, and possibly elsewhere, it is common for parties to campaign with their candidates for governor, who is announced ahead of the election. Hence, insofar as voters know in advance the likely governor they are voting for, governors may be more "directly" elected than the formal mechanics of indirect election would suggest.

At the *aimag* level, and to a lesser degree at the *soum* level, there are deconcentrated sector ministry department heads and staff (education, health, environment, etc.) who are under dual supervision by the governor and their parent ministry (or, for *soum* sector staff, by the corresponding *aimag* department).

These departments are coordinated through a Governor's Council, a body chaired by the governor comprising the heads of the departments directly under the Governor's Office, and of several other state agencies at the *aimag* level. Composition seems to be flexible. The Council usually meets every 1 to 2 weeks and establishes ad hoc working groups on specific issues.

In practice, the public financial management (PFM) framework is highly centralized, and the budgets and operations of these subnational sector departments are determined by the parent ministry. This leaves little scope for the governor to influence how local department activities are managed or local services are delivered. Supervision by the governor is thus primarily administrative.

Local Hurals

The *aimag hural* comprises 25–35 members and the *soum hural* of 15–25 members, depending on the area population. Elections are every 4 years, and there is typically a high replacement rate. About 57% of the 8,099 local *hural* representatives were elected for the first time in 2016 (Table 2).

The dominance of the Mongolian People's Party is much less marked in the *aimag hurals* than in the State *hural*. There were no data available for *soum hural* composition (Table 2).

Table 2: Elected Members by Party, 2016

Party	State *Hural*	Aimag *Hural*
Mongolian People's Party	65	528
Democratic Party	9	234
Motherland Party	–	1
Mongolian People's Revolutionary Party	1	20
National Labour Party	–	5
Independent candidates	1	21
Total elected members	**76**	**809**

– = no data available.

Source: *Mongolian Statistical Yearbook 2017.*

There are no reserved seats or other affirmative action arrangements for women or other disadvantaged or minority groups as found across South Asia. Typically, women members are a minority, with women's representation for subnational *hurals* ranging from 16% in *aimag hurals*, to 28% in *soum* and Ulaanbaatar *hurals* (Figure 2).

Figure 2: Local *Hural* Composition by Gender, 2016

REPRESENTATIVES

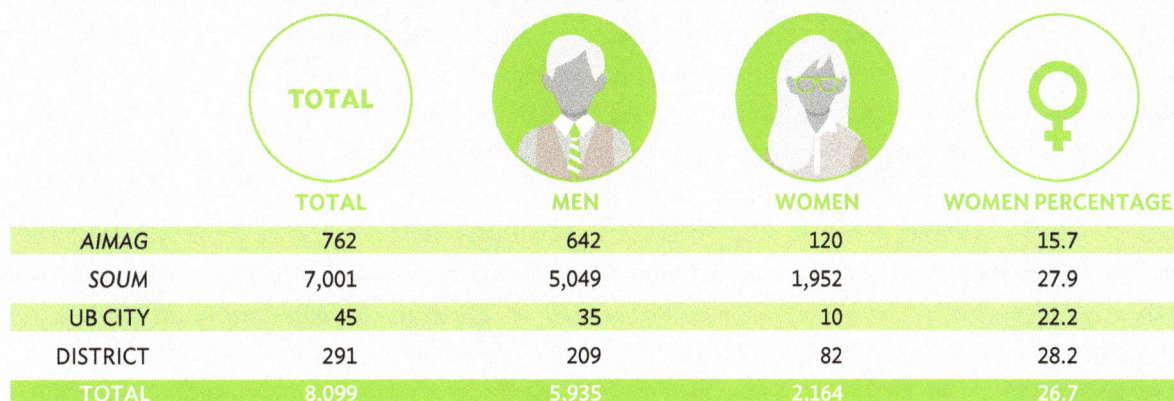

	TOTAL	MEN	WOMEN	WOMEN PERCENTAGE
AIMAG	762	642	120	15.7
SOUM	7,001	5,049	1,952	27.9
UB CITY	45	35	10	22.2
DISTRICT	291	209	82	28.2
TOTAL	8,099	5,935	2,164	26.7

PRESIDIUM MEMBERS

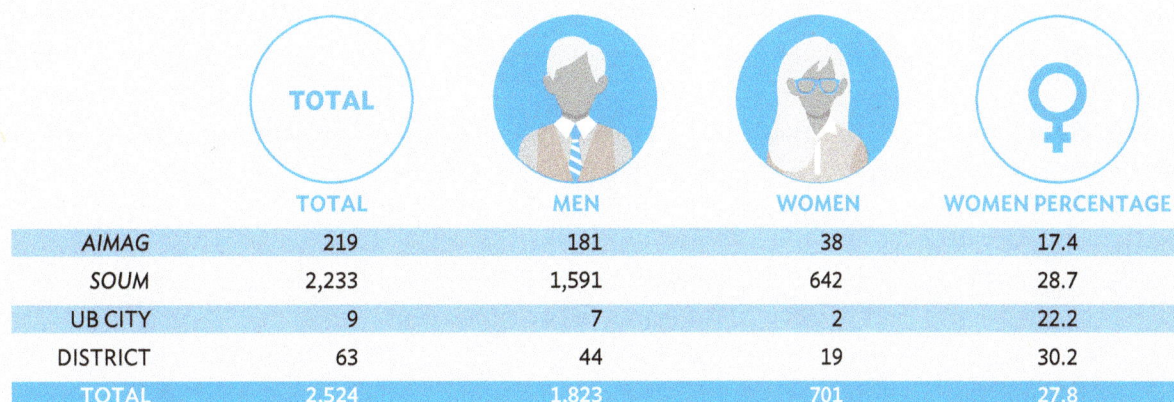

	TOTAL	MEN	WOMEN	WOMEN PERCENTAGE
AIMAG	219	181	38	17.4
SOUM	2,233	1,591	642	28.7
UB CITY	9	7	2	22.2
DISTRICT	63	44	19	30.2
TOTAL	2,524	1,823	701	27.8

CHAIRPERSONS

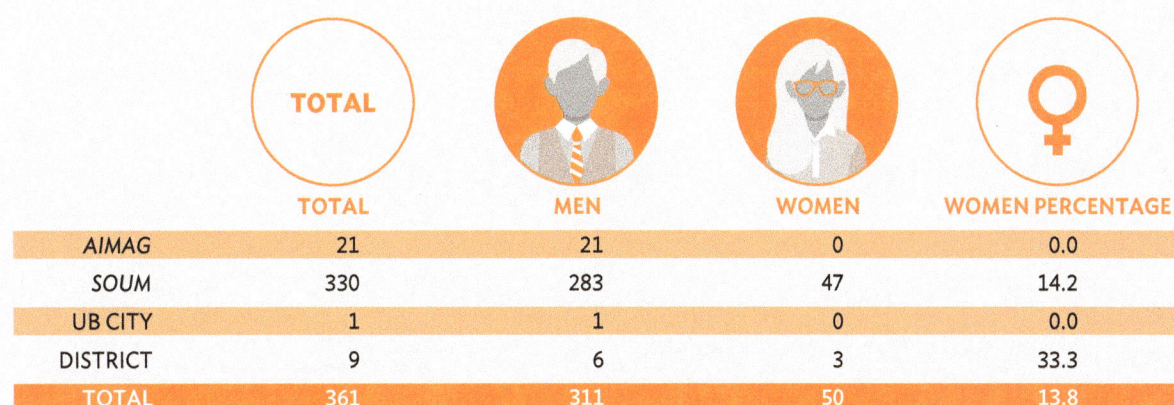

	TOTAL	MEN	WOMEN	WOMEN PERCENTAGE
AIMAG	21	21	0	0.0
SOUM	330	283	47	14.2
UB CITY	1	1	0	0.0
DISTRICT	9	6	3	33.3
TOTAL	361	311	50	13.8

aimag = province, *soum* = district, UB City = Ulaanbaatar City.

Source: UNDP and Swiss Agency for Development and Cooperation. 2016. Strengthening Representative Bodies of Mongolia Project. Ulaanbaatar.

The full *hural* usually meets 2 to 4 times a year. Both *aimag* and *soum hurals* are led by a full-time chairperson. Routine *hural* business is managed by a presidium or cabinet usually comprised of five *hural* members headed by the chair who meet several times each month. The chair and presidium members are elected by the entire *hural* following the election. Presidium members act as chairpersons of the *hural* standing committees mandated to cover specific themes—typically, budget and finance, social welfare, environment and land management, crime prevention, and law and order. However, there is no mandated standard committee setup, and *hurals* appear to have some flexibility in designating the number and scope of these standing committees. There is no budget allocation for committee activities, such as travel.

Hurals at both levels are supported by a full-time secretary with the same civil service grade as the head of the Governor's Office. *Aimag hural* secretaries are also supported by other staff, typically an officer to help organize *hural*, presidium, and committee meetings; an officer to monitor and liaise with *soum hurals*; a communications officer; and a finance officer or accountant. *Hurals* are allotted a modest annual budget to cover personnel and administration costs, which must be spent according to strict budget norms, but they have no budget of their own for discretionary or development expenditures.

Hural staffing is regulated by the central government, and *hurals* only have authority to hire contract staff on their own initiative and only then if they have discretionary funds, which is exceptional and usually only an option for SNGs with a fiscal surplus.

It is generally recognized that the *hurals* do not play their mandated policy-formulation and oversight role. The consensus is that *soum hurals* are more active than *aimag hurals*.

Box 2: The Politics of Decentralization

The present assessment of the characteristics of decentralized governance in Mongolia is based on an analysis of its institutional, administrative, and fiscal features, hence in technocratic terms.

It is important to note that decentralization reform essentially concerns the introduction of changes to the territorial distribution of state power. More specifically, it concerns the transfer of power, authority, responsibilities, and resources from higher to lower levels of government. This makes decentralization an inherently political process and not a process that reflects, or is driven merely by economic, managerial, or administrative considerations.

This publication does not include a detailed assessment of the political economy dimensions of decentralization, local governance, and local economic development in Mongolia. This is acknowledged as a limitation.

Source: Asian Development Bank.

■ A Variant: Urban Centers and Mayors

The LATUG provides a uniform framework and makes no distinctions between SNGs and their roles and powers regarding the nature of the territory or to their urban or rural contexts. This is now posing a challenge for Ulaanbaatar and emerging secondary centers.

The Law on Legal Status of Cities and Settlements was adopted in 1993. In Ulaanbaatar, this was supplemented by the Law on the Legal Status of the Capital City in 1994. The 1993 law provides a legal framework for urban centers within the territorial units legislated under the LATUG and outlined earlier. This distinguishes:

(i) Cities with national status: Cities with over 50,000 people and contributing to national socioeconomic development.

(ii) Cities with *aimag* status: A settlement with at least 15,000 people, of which the majority are employed in nonagricultural activities.

Darkhan, Erdenet, and Ulaanbaatar are defined as cities with national status, a distinction that seems to have significance primarily regarding the nature of the regional planning undertaken by the National Development Agency (NDA) and the urban planning undertaken by the Ministry of Construction and Development for these urban centers.

In national cities, the corresponding *aimag* or capital city governor is also the mayor of the city. This results in certain institutional confusion regarding the *aimag*-center *soum* authorities and their respective roles in city governance.

Several major revisions to the legislation governing the status and powers of Ulaanbaatar have been proposed, but this has been pending with the State *hural* for several years now. One reported obstacle is this would require a constitutional amendment since Chapter 4 of the Constitution puts the capital city and *aimags* on an equal legal footing.

■ Mongolian Association of Local Authorities

The Mongolian Association of Local Authorities (MALA) is a nongovernment organization that provides support services for *aimag* and *soum hurals*.[2] It also plays an occasional role in policy consultation and advocacy, convenes workshops, and organizes training events. Training events are generally run by the staff of the National Academy of Governance (NAOG).

The efficacy of the MALA is constrained by lack of funding and staff (the MALA only has an executive director and one support staff) and by the political partisanship that permeates local *hurals* as much as it does at the central government level.

---

[2]   The Mongolian Association of Local Authorities was originally set up with support from the Swedish International Development Agency.

2. Subnational Government Resources

■ Human Resources

General

There are several categories of human resources within the dual SNG structures.

(i)   The elected chairperson and other representatives on the SNG *hurals* are all part-time except for presidium members.

(ii) Secretariat staff working in support of the SNG *hural* and its chairperson and presidium.

(iii) The elected SNG governors and their deputies.

(iv) Staff working in departments directly and solely under the authority of the SNG governor.

(v)   Staff working in deconcentrated sector departments and other agencies deployed to SNG level who operate under the dual authority of the governor and their central ministry or agency.

The number of civil servants deployed to subnational level is around 193,500 people (60% women);[3] while elected *hural* members number 8,099 for *aimags* and *soums* combined. In one *aimag* (the smallest, Govisumber, population: 17,500), the total number of civil servants in all categories was reported to be 480, not including 870 teachers, health, and social workers, or 1:36 persons.[4] This is a high ratio compared to many other Asian countries. There is a substantial number of personnel working at both *aimag* and *soum* levels in support of the *hurals*, under the governor, and in the deconcentrated sector departments and agencies. Table 3 compares typical staffing levels of the *soum* with those of the lowest level SNGs in other Asian countries.

Table 3: Typical Staffing at Lowest Subnational Government Levels in Asia

Country	Number of Staff
Mongolia: *Soums*	• Hural Secretary • Governor and deputy governor and 6–10 staff in the Governor's Office • 5–6 sector department heads and staff • Total: 20–30 staff
Kazakhstan: Akimats	3–10 staff depending on population size
Viet Nam: Communes	10–15 staff
Bangladesh: Union Parishads	5–10 staff

Source: Asian Development Bank (based on the research by the authors).

[3] For employment statistics, see Mongolian Statistical Information Service. http://www.1212.mn/tables.aspx?TBL_ID=DT_NSO_0400_040V1.

[4] Statistics on the total number of civil servants in other *aimags* suggest similarly high ratios elsewhere in Mongolia.

Human Resource Management

There is no separate civil service cadre or regime for SNG personnel who are governed by the national Civil Service Law, the most recently amended version of which came into effect in January 2019 or the Labour Law (1999), which governs terms of employment. There is a central Civil Service Council (CSC) under the State *hural* to formulate and oversee policy and procedures, performance monitoring, and training programs for public servants of all categories at the central and SNG level.

Within this legal framework, there is a degree of local control over SNG personnel, at least for staff in the *hural* secretariat and the departments under the SNG governor. In contrast, governors use their dual oversight role over staff in deconcentrated sector departments, while the central sector ministries play the main role.

Based on anecdotal evidence, there appears to be some degree of mobility within the system. *Soum hural* secretaries and teachers can stand for election and become *soum hural* chairs. *Soum hural* chairs can then become *soum* governors, *soum* governors can become *aimag* deputy governors, and *aimag* deputy governors can join the Cabinet Secretariat.

Mongolia has faced challenges in developing an adequate legal and regulatory framework for its civil servants despite amendments to the Civil Service and the Election Laws and enhanced powers for the independent CSC.

One reason for the recent Civil Service Law amendments (supported by UNDP–Canadian International Development Agency, Appendix 2) was to provide greater protection to the civil service from the long-standing problem of political interference. This manifests in increased turnover among senior officials at central and SNG levels, especially following elections, and increased complaints to the CSC. There are chronic tensions and staff dismissals within SNG administrations, allegedly due to conflicting party loyalties. This undermines morale, good governance, and SNG performance.[5]

The revised Civil Service Law contains measures for reform that would reinforce a career-based civil service regime with minimum years of service for different grades and promotion to senior posts. This could be achieved by further strengthening the CSC and by introducing sanctions on supervisors for unfair dismissals, and obliging supervisors to reimburse salary costs to unfairly dismissed staff. However, it is unclear how effective these measures would be. Under the new law, the number of local civil servants who may sit on an SNG *hural* is capped at 30% to reduce their dominance and create space for representatives of other sectors of society.

---

[5] CSC statistics suggest that some 7,500 civil servants voluntarily leave the civil service annually. See UNDP. 2018. *Towards a Professional and Citizen-centred Civil Service in Mongolia.* Ulaanbaatar.

Human Resource Support and Training

Routine support and backstopping. The Department of Local Administration (DLA) of the Cabinet Secretariat provides regular support and policy and legal briefing to *aimag* governors and staff and *hural* secretariat staff through workshops and field visits. It also arranges for staff training. The *aimag* administration and *aimag hural* secretariat provide support to *soum* bodies (Box 3).

Box 3: The Vertical Support and Backstopping Chain

Staff from the six main departments under the *aimag* Governor's Office (Public Administration, Finance and Treasury, Development Policy, Monitoring and Evaluation, Social Policy and Legal Affairs) provide periodic support to the corresponding personnel in the *soum* governors' offices through (i) periodic briefings on government policy and regulatory changes, (ii) occasional training sessions, and (iii) ad hoc telephone help-line support for specific queries and visits by *soum* staff.

Similarly, staff in other central government department and agency branches at the *aimag* level, which have dual reporting lines to the Governor's Office and their parent ministries in Ulaanbaatar, such as the procurement or land agencies, also provide support to *soums* in their respective areas.

The *aimag hural* secretariat staff (with 10–12 persons) typically provide periodic training to *soum hural* members and the Secretary through periodic joint briefing or training sessions with *aimag* governor staffs on topics such as finance or planning and occasional events where they provide briefings on legal and administrative matters pertaining to the *hural* and its role and operations. There is also a civic participation officer on the *aimag hural* staff who is mainly engaged in surveys to solicit citizen feedback on *aimag* initiatives. This person could potentially play a role in supporting *soum hural* members in their representational roles.

All support activities are planned and coordinated through the *aimag* governor's council of department heads.

Source: Asian Development Bank (based on consultations with local government officials in Govisumber and Darkhan Province).

Formal training. The NAOG grew out of the former Communist Party training school and is the national training institute for civil servants and public management under the authority of the Cabinet Secretariat. It provides five to six trainers in public administration for SNG personnel in one of the following ways at the Academy of Management's Ulaanbaatar campus:

(i)   Master's programs for *aimag* personnel (18 months)

(ii)   Diploma programs for *aimag* and *soum* personnel (8 months)

(iii) Certificate programs for *aimag* and *soum* personnel (3 months)

However, its effectiveness is somewhat limited. Only a few officials can attend given the relatively high cost, key officials cannot take such long periods off work to attend, and training materials are generic and not always relevant to the tasks and challenges that SNG officials must undertake. More recently, these materials are said to be improving.

The NAOG also provides ad hoc short-term training services for capacity development programs. For example, NAOG is engaged in the UNDP–SDC *hural* project training *aimag* officials as trainers for *hural* representatives.[6]

Ulaanbaatar has established a separate training center for Ulaanbaatar personnel, catering to batches of 40 staff at a time, especially for those at district and *khoroo* levels.

Financing

As Mongolia has moved to reform public finance after its socialist phase, the fiscal relations between central and subnational governments have vacillated somewhat—from the wide fiscal autonomy enjoyed by the SNGs in the 1990s, which led to the Public Sector Financial Management Law of 2002, and a radical recentralization of fiscal powers and public expenditure management and then to the Budget Law of 2012. The Budget Law of 2012 has swung the pendulum back toward a modest degree of fiscal decentralization by introducing several important innovations:

(i) **A modest decentralization of functions.** Under Article 58, there is a move to more clearly define the devolved service delivery functions of *aimags* and *soums* and provide a list of specific though still modest responsibilities for the *soum* level. Under Article 61, there is a move to delegate basic education and primary health responsibilities to the *aimag* level, to be managed on a contractual basis with respective line ministries and financed through special fiscal transfers.

(ii) **Reassignment of revenues.** Under Article 23, there has been an assignment of a modest set of tax and nontax revenues for local governments, reducing revenue-sharing between levels and assigning the bulk of mineral tax revenues to central government, thereby allowing a potentially more effective and equitable fiscal transfer system.

(iii) **A discretionary investment fund.** Under Article 59, a General Local Development Fund was established to finance formula-based grants for SNGs. This constitutes a significant policy breakthrough in SNG financing arrangements and, for the first time, allows a modest volume of flexible financing to respond to local priorities.

(iv) **Empowerment of SNG authorities and citizen engagement.** Under Articles 64–68, *aimag* and *soum* governors are mandated to formulate budget proposals for submission to *hurals* and implement approved budgets. *Aimag* and *soum hurals* are mandated to debate and approve local budgets and oversee execution, conduct hearings on SNG governors' reports, and inform the public. The public can provide input to *hural* discussions regarding budget preparation, and budgets must be made available to the public in a transparent manner.

Despite these reforms, the SNG financing framework is still strongly shaped by the socialist legacy, whereby SNGs at *aimag* and *soum* levels are categorized as being in fiscal deficit or surplus, and where even local spending is subject to strict ex ante central controls (Box 4). This undermines the quality and equity of service delivery and often discourages local civic engagement with SNGs, limiting their ability to respond to such engagement.

---

[6] UNDP-SDC. 2016. *Strengthening of Local Self-Governing Bodies in Mongolia.* Ulaanbaatar.

Box 4: The Inherited Public Finance Paradigm: Surplus and Deficit Transfer Arrangements

Surplus and deficit transfer arrangements are a common fiscal paradigm, especially in socialist or transition countries. Their functions are:

- Subnational governments (SNGs) prepare their budget estimates for their revenues and expenditures for the next fiscal year and submit them to the central level for review.
- Where projected revenues exceed expenditures, there is an arrangement for some part of the surplus to revert to the central government for redistribution to other SNGs.
- Where projected expenditures exceed revenues (as is the usual case), the central government will cut these back to approved levels, often in negotiation with the concerned SNGs, and then allocate a deficit grant to cover the difference.

Several problems have been documented in other former socialist economies that have inherited a similar intergovernmental fiscal system:

- They greatly weaken incentives for local budget preparation discipline, priority-setting, and local revenue-raising.
- They push up de facto budget priority making and cutting to central government officials who are not in the best position to make such choices.
- They deprive central government of resources to ensure horizontal equity across SNGs.

Overall, they tend to encourage nontransparent central-local deal-making and patronage. In Viet Nam, where a similar model long prevailed, local officials occasionally referred to these arrangements as the "beg and receive" system.

Source: Asian Development Bank.

3. Central Policy and Oversight Bodies

■ Cabinet Secretariat

General

In Mongolia, there is no Ministry of Local Government or Home Affairs or similar body with a clear SNG oversight and policy mandate as in other countries. At the central government level, this role is to some extent played by the DLA within the Cabinet Secretariat (CS/DLA), alongside other central ministries and agencies. The roles of CS/DLA include

(i)   issuing central government regulations and directives to SNGs, although it does not appear to actively propose policy or legal reform initiatives regarding SNGs;

(ii)   organizing and financing SNG staff training, usually undertaken through the Academy of Management or MALA (CS/DLA has no staff for this purpose);

(iii)   monitoring compliance through the Monitoring, Evaluation, Inspection and Audit Department (MEIAD), and reporting to the Prime Minister and to Parliament. MEIAD has established *aimag*-level units of three to four staff in each *aimag* to strengthen its monitoring role; this is the first such CS/DLA staff posted at the SNG level;

(iv)   convening SNG governors for policy briefings and debriefings to support national program implementation and address local or regional crises or natural disasters such as the seasonal *dzuds*;[7] and

---

[7]   Severe winter following a lean summer causing extensive death of cattle.

(v)   liaising with other parts of the central government on behalf of the SNGs (e.g., persuading MOF to allow *aimags* to procure within their powers and facilitating *aimag* negotiations with sector ministries over their contracts for delegated functions).

The Vertical Supervision Chain

General administrative supervision of *aimag* governors and their staff and *aimag hurals* is provided by the CS/DLA. In turn, *aimag* governors and staff similarly supervise *soum* governors and staff, and *aimag hurals* and staff supervise *soum hurals*.

Supervision and inspection of SNG budget and financial management are undertaken by different MOF divisions that operate through their *aimag* finance department staff under the *aimag* governor.

(i)   **Governors.** *Aimag* governors report to the Cabinet Secretariat on *aimag* SNG activities generally and on local implementation of national programs every 6 months. Based on these reports and other surveys conducted by other agencies (anticorruption, civil service, NGO, and other assessments), the Cabinet Secretariat then makes an overall assessment and ranking of *aimag* performance, which is submitted to the Cabinet. The three worst-performing *aimag* governors receive a salary penalty, but no other sanctions or rewards appear to be applied. The Cabinet Secretariat organizes periodic workshops for *aimag* governors where these reports and related issues are discussed and lessons exchanged. There is a similar exercise whereby *soum* governors report to *aimag* governors, and *soum* performance assessments are made by the *aimag* monitoring and evaluation department. However, it appears there is some variation in these arrangements between *aimags*.

(ii)   ***Hurals.*** It is sometimes argued that local *hurals*, insofar as they are legally defined under the LATUG as self-governing bodies, are outside central government supervision. This is not entirely correct. All *aimag* and *soum hural* activities and meeting minutes are subject to review by the CS/DLA and by the *aimag* governor. All *hural* resolutions and decisions on local policy matters and local regulations are submitted to the Ministry of Justice and the CS/DLA for review. If they are deemed unlawful, these decisions or resolutions may be revoked or submitted to the State Inspection Agency for action.

■ Ministry of Finance

There is no dedicated SNG finance department within MOF to act as a focal point for subnational finance issues.[8] However, central MOF divisions and departments each provide support and supervision to their corresponding *aimag* departments in the different areas of budgeting and public financial management. The *aimag* finance departments provide support and supervision to their counterparts at *soum* level.

The MOF online treasury management information system provides a mechanism for reporting and central oversight of SNG transactions and there is a separate management information system for the LDF (Section 2), which is being upgraded with support from the Sustainable Livelihoods Project Phase 3 (SLP3).

---

[8]   A small, two-person Local Development Fund Unit was established under the National Democratic Party government to oversee SNG use of the Local Development Fund, but this was abolished by the incoming Mongolian People's Party government in 2016, and the functions incorporated into those of the larger Budget Consolidation Division of the Fiscal Policy Department.

Since 2016, MOF has been testing a nationwide performance assessment mechanism for all 330 *soums*, where high-performing *soums* are rewarded with an increment to their basic LDF allocation (Appendix 1). Aside from MOF supervision, SNGs are subject to a range of other external audit controls.

■ Mongolian National Audit Office

The Mongolian National Audit Office (MNAO) is the supreme auditing authority established under the Audit Law and reports to the State *hural*. It has a national office in Ulaanbaatar and offices in each of the *aimags* that have been under central MNAO authority since 2014. Previously they were under the *aimag* governors. *Aimag* national audit offices (NAOs) each have a chief auditor, audit manager, and field audit staff totaling 11–12 people who report to the local audit section of the central MNAO.

The MNAO is building up *aimag* capacities to plan, implement, and follow up and report on the audits undertaken, but they face constraints affecting their capacity and independence.

A national audit working group has been established to review the policy, legal, and regulatory framework for government audits and to address other factors affecting both the capacity and independence of the MNAO.

The *aimag* MNAO offices conduct financial, performance, and compliance audits of all government budget entities (as defined in the Budget Law), including the *aimag* and *soum* administrations (as general budget governors for their areas) and government facilities such as schools and hospitals (direct budget governors). Typically, each *aimag* MNAO office conducts 200–300 such audits each year, between the third week of January until June. Given the various constraints, only a fraction of SNGs and other local budget entities are subject to audit in any one year.

■ State Inspection Agency

The State Inspection Agency was established under the Law on State Supervision and Inspection (2003, revised 2010) with a wide-ranging mandate, including but not limited to:

(i)   inspection of financial management and legal compliance of all state organizations;

(ii)   monitoring implementation of national laws, regulations, and directives; and

(iii) monitoring policy and national program implementation in transport, education, health, social, and cultural areas, and evaluation of the quality of services provided.

The State Inspection Agency employs inspectors at central and SNG levels. However, under Articles 8 and 12 of the Law on State Supervision and Inspection, SNG governors and SNG *hurals* are also empowered to undertake such inspections themselves under the authority of the law, including reciprocal oversight.

There is an apparent degree of institutional overlap and duplication in work between these activities and the National Audit Offices audits.

4. Accountabilities to Citizens and Civil Society

Article 16 of the Constitution enshrines the rights of citizens to participate in public affairs, both through the election of *hural* representatives and through direct engagement with the state and its officials, and for free association.

■ General Citizen Engagement

There is a range of legal provisions for citizen engagement with the state and for state transparency to citizens (Box 5). One national NGO claims there are 110 laws in different sectors that promote or mandate citizen involvement, but these are far from fully implemented. Since 1991, there has been considerable impetus from development partners active in promoting practices for greater citizen engagement with the government and extending considerable support to town hall meetings and similar initiatives (e.g., the United States Agency for International Development, The Asia Foundation, Open Society Forum, Mercy Corps).

Box 5: Selected Legal Provisions to Allow Citizen Engagement and Transparency

- Law on Deliberative Polling (2017)
- Law on Information Transparency and the Right to Information (June 2011)
- Law on Managing and Preventing Conflict of Public and Private Interest in Public Service (January 2012)
- Law on Budget (Article 6.5) amended to improve implementation to enable citizen participation for greater transparency (December 2011)
- Law on Glass Account (2014)
- Law on Public Polling (2015)
- Law on Development Policy and Planning (2015)
- Regulation on Ensuring Budget and Financial Transparency (January 2012)
- Regulation on Contracting out Government Goods and Services to NGOs (Government Resolution No. 165 of 21 March 2016)
- Criteria on Transparency (Government Resolution No. 143, 2009)
- Public Procurement Law (revised, 2019)

Source: Asian Development Bank.

The following laws are worth highlighting.

(i)   The 2015 Law of Development Policy and Planning and the subsidiary 2016 Regulation on Development Policy and Planning mandate the need to secure both citizen and local *hural* input to and public discussion of plans and policies.

(ii)   The 2017 Deliberative Polling Law aims to introduce mandatory citizen polling, not only for national constitutional amendments and major legislation but also for local planning, although it is too early to say what impact this may have.[9]

---

[9]   This emerged from advisory work sponsored by The Asia Foundation involving Professor James S. Fishkin of the Stanford Center for Deliberative Democracy.

(iii) The recent Glass Account Law mandates that SNGs undertake a wide range of disclosure, especially around the local budget and procurement processes. However, this seems to be mainly online disclosure and may have limited utility for ordinary citizens.

(iv) The Public Procurement Law opens opportunities for ordinary citizens and NGOs to be involved in both the selection of contractors and monitoring implementation. Major limits to effective citizen involvement here lie in the lack of clear guidelines for such involvement and the precondition that bid evaluation committee members must hold an A3 Certificate in procurement proficiency, a qualification not easy to acquire. Any involvement requires a large time commitment and probably holds little appeal to people other than community members who may be directly affected by a particular project.

(v) At the SNG level, the Budget Law and the subsidiary MOF LDF regulation make it mandatory that annual planning for the LDF be based on an exercise where all households are polled for their views and priorities and that all such proposals then be subject to discussion and vote at a *bagh or khoroo* meeting. A necessary condition for any project to be funded by the LDF is that it has emerged as a citizen priority from this process. The evidence suggests this provision is widely complied with, although at times in a rather mechanical manner. It is also sometimes subject to manipulation and misuse.

(vi) The LATUG provides for regular *bagh* or *khoroo* consultations. At the *bagh* level, meetings of voting adults are held five or six times a year to discuss issues of local interest and to submit proposals to the *hural*. The *hural* member attends these meetings, which are convened by the elected *bagh* governor. The LATUG also mandates governors to report to citizens at public meetings (Govisumber *aimag* governor claims to hold two such public meetings annually to report on activities and solicit feedback, answer queries, and hear complaints).

Most SNGs in Mongolia maintain a Facebook page, which is said to be an effective forum for disclosure to citizens and for citizens to raise issues and ask questions.

Mongolia is one of a group of 80 countries that have subscribed to the Open Government Partnership, in which it has made commitments embedded in a National Action Plan. Several of these commitments pertain to a more open and citizen-responsive government at local levels.[10]

■ Civil Society Engagement

Associations of citizens are often referred to interchangeably as NGOs or civil society organizations (CSOs) in Mongolia. They are regulated primarily by the Law on NGOs (1997), the Civil Code (2002), the Law on Regulating Public Demonstrations and Meetings (1994), the Law on Regulating Resolution of Citizens Applications and Grievances (1995), and the Law on State Registration of Legal Entities (2015). Box 6 summarizes the roles of NGOs and CSOs per the NGO law.[11]

---

[10]   Commitments made by Mongolia can be found at https://www.opengovpartnership.org/countries/mongolia.

[11]   Drafted originally with support from The Asia Foundation.

Box 6: Roles Accorded to Nongovernment Organizations and Civil Society Organizations

The Law on NGOs (1997) distinguishes between organizations operating solely for the benefit of members and those operating for public benefit. It specifies the preconditions for their registration. From 2018, registration was switched from the Ministry of Justice to central or subnational government (SNG) branches of the State Inspection Agency.

The provisions under the law for NGO relations with the state and with SNGs are embodied in Article 9: Relations between State Bodies and Nongovernmental Organizations:

1. The State shall protect the legitimate rights of nongovernmental organizations.
2. Nongovernmental organizations shall be independent of state bodies.
3. The State may support, financially and otherwise, activities of nongovernmental organizations.
4. Information relating to activities of State bodies, unless classified as State secrets, shall be open to nongovernmental organizations.
5. Nongovernmental organizations may be involved in drafting and implementing the decisions to be taken by legislative and executive authorities.
6. Nongovernmental organizations may make public statements about their positions on decisions taken by the State.

Source: Law on NGOs (1997).

Formally registered NGOs are mainly urban-based. They are often not functional, although there is an increasing trend in the number of local groups. A recent ADB report states that:[12]

> As of June 2018, 17,634 CSOs were formally registered. This includes 15,241 CSOs for public benefit and 2,393 mutual benefit CSOs. While the total number of registered CSOs is high, only a few have regular and systematic operations. Over 80% are based in the capital, and the remaining are registered at the local (*aimag*) level. Locally based organizations are increasing in number and have strengthened their capacity over time. Community-based organizations are mostly run on a voluntary basis, are generally small, and do not have full-time staff. Medium-sized civil society organizations typically have two to five regular staff and volunteers. Women figured prominently at both the membership and leadership levels, accounting for over 80% of the staff members.

One reason for the increase in local groups is the expansion of mining activities. Community groups are forming to address the social and environmental issues that arise out of these activities.

There is also a strong tradition of social organization in rural areas, given the imperatives of livestock and pasture range management. These groups, while often not formally registered as NGOs, do raise their concerns and interests with their SNGs, for example, around the annual planning activities for the LDF (Box 7). This has been supported in some cases by development partners, such as SDC's support to pastureland user groups under the Green Gold project.

[12] ADB. 2018. *Civil Society Brief: Mongolia*. Manila.

Box 7: Two Nongovernment Organization and Civil Society Initiatives to Monitor Subnational Governments

The **Open Society Foundation (Mongolia)** conducts a regular biannual survey of *aimag* performance in their implementation of national policy and legislation on transparency and disclosure. This is contracted out through local nongovernment organizations (NGOs). It provides support to local NGOs in 20 *aimags* to assess the accountability of subnational government (SNG) expenditures, the implementation of the Glass Account provisions, and the use of public hearings.

The **Economic Policy and Competitiveness Research Center** conducts annual assessments for the *Aimag Competitiveness Report* and the *Ulaanbaatar Competitiveness Report*. This is supported by GIZ, TAF, and the Mongolian National Chamber of Commerce and Industry. This assessment uses secondary sources and direct surveys. It rates *aimags* on several dimensions and includes measures of government efficiency related to budget performance and business legislation. The box figure shows government efficiency rankings for 2018.

This is an extremely important and potentially useful exercise. However, there are questions around some of the criteria currently used, such as the extent of *aimag* budget surplus, which appears to reflect contextual factors over which SNG authorities have little control, and which also do not necessarily reflect SNG performance.

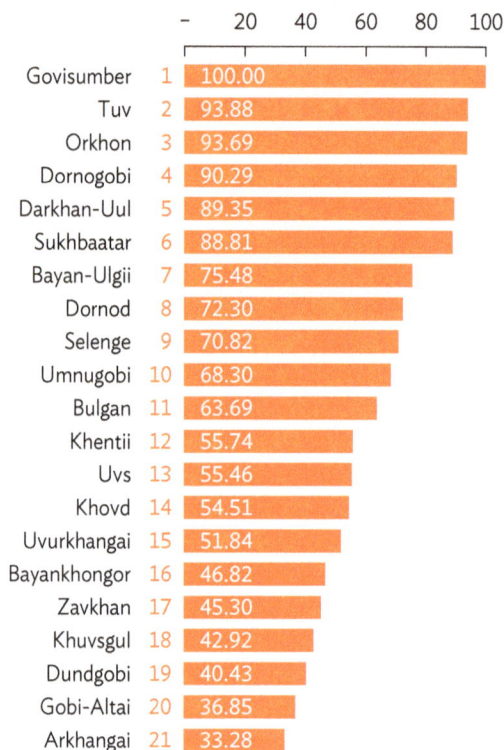

Govisumber	1	100.00
Tuv	2	93.88
Orkhon	3	93.69
Dornogobi	4	90.29
Darkhan-Uul	5	89.35
Sukhbaatar	6	88.81
Bayan-Ulgii	7	75.48
Dornod	8	72.30
Selenge	9	70.82
Umnugobi	10	68.30
Bulgan	11	63.69
Khentii	12	55.74
Uvs	13	55.46
Khovd	14	54.51
Uvurkhangai	15	51.84
Bayankhongor	16	46.82
Zavkhan	17	45.30
Khuvsgul	18	42.92
Dundgobi	19	40.43
Gobi-Altai	20	36.85
Arkhangai	21	33.28

GIZ = Deutsche Gesellschaft für Internationale Zusammenarbeit, TAF = The Asia Foundation.

Source: Economic Policy and Competitiveness Research Center. 2017. *Mongolia: Provincial Competitiveness Report 2017*. Ulaanbaatar.

B. Local Development Role for Subnational Governments in Mongolia

The SNG institutions outlined above enjoy certain comparative institutional advantages and disadvantages in the role they can play to promote local development in their jurisdictions.

1. Policy Stance toward Decentralization

Government policy on decentralization within the institutional framework outlined above has evolved since 1991. The details of intergovernmental fiscal relations policy were examined in Section 2. In general:

(i)   From 1991 to 2002, SNGs were granted considerable autonomy and discretion.

(ii)   From 2002 to 2013, powers were centralized, and SNGs were essentially agents of the central government. This arose from concerns about local policymaking, public finance, and budget management, which had arisen during the previous period.

(iii) From 2013 until the present, there has been a gradual move back to assigning responsibilities and resources to SNGs following the passage of the new Budget Law (2012).

Until recently, there has been no clear policy statement by the government articulating a vision of decentralization and the role of SNGs. However, a first statement was issued in June 2016, as Government Resolution No. 350. The overarching goals and principles are presented in Box 8.

Box 8: **Goal, Principles, and Directions of the Decentralization Policy**

The main goal of the State Policy on Decentralization is to foster transparent, accountable, and good governance and economic and social development based on citizen participation and to create conditions for more effective and accessible public service delivery to citizens by implementing decentralization in Mongolia in a sequenced, coherent, and comprehensive manner.

Chapter 2 of Government Resolution No. 350 states:

2.2 The following directions shall be adhered to when implementing the State Policy on Decentralization:

2.2.1 Re-allocation of some functions of central government and local self-governing and administrative bodies related to common public services to local administrations which directly interact with citizens at lower and intermediate levels, without overlapping, except for those of the courts, armed forces, police, intelligence, and State security and emergency.

2.2.2 Implement flexible investment and tax policies towards ensuring local economic independence and improving local development funds.

2.2.3 Adequate financial resources are allocated to central and local self-governing and administrative organisations to enable the performance of functions assigned by law.

2.2.4 Create a mechanism that conducts common and specific timely measures when needed to ensure the cooperation between the central government and the local governing and administrative organisations.

2.2.5 Ensure coherence between the implementation of functions and the accountability and monitoring of the corresponding government levels.

2.2.6 Some government functions assigned by law to be carried out by public-private partnerships and nongovernment organizations can be transferred based on the principle of fair competition.

2.3 When implementing the State decentralization policy, the following principles shall be applied:

2.3.1 Coherent, comprehensive, and integrated

2.3.2 Systematic

2.3.3 Based on good international practice, scientific theory, methodology, and analysis

2.3.4 Involves central government and local self-governing and administrative organisations at all levels

2.3.5 Public services are to be accessible, efficient, and effective

2.3.6 Ensure openness, accountability, and citizen participation

Source: Chapter 2 of Government of Mongolia. 2016. Government Resolution No. 350. Ulaanbaatar.

Part 5 of this resolution states that the Cabinet Secretariat is charged with ensuring interministerial collaboration to develop and implement this policy framework. However, no interministerial body has been set up for this purpose, and it is unrealistic to expect the Cabinet to perform this role.

A State *hural* working group of national members of Parliament has been recently established to review proposed amendments to Chapter 4 of the Constitution and the LATUG and make recommendations for reform. This exercise was prompted by consultations on legal impediments to good local governance organized by the Cabinet Secretariat through the UNDP–SDC *hural* project (Appendix 2). Some areas proposed for possible legislative change relate to SNG governor–*hural* relations and accountabilities, SNG service delivery responsibilities generally, the *aimag–soum* division of responsibilities, and SNG financing arrangements.

2. Overall Framework for Subnational Governance: Issues

■ Policy and Legal Framework and Oversight

There is a lack of a central ministerial focus for policy making, implementation, and monitoring, for matters related to SNGs, and for coordination across powerful ministries with a voice in Cabinet. It is unclear to what extent there is government and political buy-in to the strategy in the 2016 Government Resolution. This may be compounded by weakness within the SNGs, especially *hurals,* in articulating common policy issues and recommendations to central government. Nevertheless, an opportunity for reform is now represented by the current State *hural* working group.

That the SNGs are subject to a high degree of central oversight and control by different parts of central government is positive, however, there are trade-offs:

(i)   Such a high level of central oversight poses a considerable workload for SNGs, especially given their staff shortages.[13]

(ii)   The fear of central sanctions coupled with often unclear guidelines can lead to hesitation or inaction. This has been seen with the LDF, where *soums* have been fearful of audit sanctions for investing in legitimate and important projects such as refurbishing a health facility belonging to a sector ministry, but where it was unclear if they were prescribed by regulation. Thus, they chose other projects.

(iii) The MNAO audits of SNGs appear to be of uneven quality. This may be due to inadequate guidance on procedures and standards.

■ Subnational Government Institutions

Generally, there seems to be agreement on the need to review the LATUG legal framework to clarify gray areas surrounding the respective roles and relations between SNG governors and *hurals,* which appear to be weakening horizontal accountabilities within the SNGs.

Local *hurals* all too often play a symbolic role and act as rubber stamps for proposed budgets and budget execution reports submitted to them by the executive. This is exacerbated by several factors:

(i)   The PFM and sector norm framework are highly centralized, which virtually excludes any local flexibility in the way budgets can be prepared or executed, leaving little to be discussed locally. This greatly hampers the local executive and the *hurals.* Anecdotal evidence suggests that in most cases, *hurals* and SNG governors are united in their desire to exercise local adaptation to central programs and are frustrated with the inflexibility of local sector departments and their parent ministries.

(ii)   The resources of the *hural,* presidium, and standing committees are limited, which hinders travel across wide areas to visit service delivery facilities or other local sites, monitor service delivery, consult with officials, and consolidate local priorities.

---

[13] For example, in Bayantal *soum,* there are only two accountants for 10 budget units, who must deal not only with the routine management and accounting but also respond to and prepare reports for the various oversight bodies.

(iii) The limited support and training provided to local *hural* members further hinders their ability to tackle budget and PFM issues in an informed, analytical manner.

(iv) These issues are exacerbated by the part-time role of most local *hural* members and by the high turnover at elections.

The SNG governors are often severely constrained by the centralized PFM arrangements and can face difficulties in exerting real control or coordination across deconcentrated sector departments and staff. The effectiveness of personnel in both branches of SNGs is compromised by relatively weak guidance, support, training, and political partisanship. Thus, while SNGs in Mongolia enjoy substantial human resource endowments, their effectiveness is limited by the broader political, policy, and legal frameworks within which they operate.

■ Citizen Engagement and Downward Accountabilities

Despite the plethora of legal texts that make formal provision for local engagement, there is often little information or guidance for SNG officials or public information on how to implement their provisions.

At the SNG level, it is arguable that the limited local decision-making authority, other than for the LDF, acts to discourage citizen and NGO engagement with local authorities since the local authorities are usually unable to respond. This is also seen in the management of individual facilities such as schools, where parent–teacher associations usually play a passive role since school directors enjoy little flexibility in budget allocation due to the tight central budget norms imposed.

NGOs often appear not to fully realize the constraints under which SNGs operate, especially their limited budgetary discretion, and have unrealistic expectations of their responsiveness.

Some national NGOs and CSOs feel that the expansion of NGOs has led to a free-for-all, undermining the image of civil society.[14] They argue the need for revisions to the NGO law and tightening registration requirements to ensure only those with a clear, legitimate agenda and with financial resources be accorded NGO status. One or more proposals for revised drafts are pending at the Justice Ministry. Progress is said to be slow.

3. The Role of Subnational Governments and the Levers of Local Public Action: Preview

To fulfill their role, SNGs in Mongolia have a number of levers for public action at their disposal. These are conferred through the various legal instruments referred to in this publication. The effectiveness of some will be reviewed in the following sections. These levers comprise a set of service delivery responsibilities and regulatory and convening powers. Box 9 summarizes the levers employed by SNGs in Mongolia.

---

[14] Some NGO representatives claim that the increased use of social media has lessened citizen interest in more time-consuming collective activity with fellow citizens.

How far these potential advantages are realized and whether these levers can be deployed effectively is dependent on the local capacity of SNG institutions, the policy and procedural framework within which they must operate, the human and financial resources at their disposal and, crucially, information resources.

Box 9: Delivery of Local Public Services

Socioeconomic Services and Investments

Socioeconomic services and investments are based on devolved or delegated functional mandates and financed by the respective subnational government (SNG) budgets. These entail public spending on local services and infrastructure (public or merit goods), in which the private sector will underinvest. They include the following:

- Education, health, water, and other social services and infrastructure to improve human well-being and the development of human capital delivery and access.
- Economic services and investments to promote local economic development (e.g., roads, industrial areas, power generation or distribution, pasture improvement and fencing, farm extension, and veterinary services).
- Spending directed preferentially to local suppliers and contractors or local communities in the case of small public works.
- Services where SNGs may leverage their ownership of public assets. As part of the socialist heritage, SNGs often own public assets and property, which is currently unused or underused and which can be put to good developmental use. For example, state land, which could be allocated for business development, waste disposal, and public parks; and former military buildings, which could be converted into office space, schools, and cultural centers.
- Welfare payments and transfers.

Administration of social transfers includes civil registration services (payments to pensioners, military veterans, disabled, etc.). Citizens can register births, deaths, marriages, and residency either directly at the State Registry office at the *aimag* (province) level (a deconcentrated branch of the General Authority of the State Registry) or through the SNG Governor's Office at any level.

Regulatory Powers

- Issuing business permits, for example, trade-specific permits to open and operate a business, to be issued by the sector department concerned (only in Ulaanbaatar and at the *aimag* level).
- Issuing land-use permits and rules, for example, land use and ownership or possession titles for citizens and businesses in rural or urban areas (to be issued by SNG governors at all levels, as they exercise discretion on these approvals).
- Facilitating legally mandated registration and access to registry documents for both citizens and businesses through opening local one-stop-service shops, business centers, or other channels.
- Ensuring proper zoning of economic and land-use activity to ease congestion, mitigate pollution, and promote economies of agglomeration.
- Ensuring control over natural resource extraction.
- Supporting local collective arrangements, for example, pasture management by herders.
- Powers to provide incentives through decisions made according or extending land-use permits and invoking delegated powers to subsidize nighttime power tariffs for citizens or businesses.

Convening Powers

Convening powers bring together stakeholders to plan or make decisions on local development issues for which they ordinarily may not meet or communicate, for example:

- groups of herders and farmers meet to agree on a common land or pasture management issue;
- groups of businesspeople meet to agree on a joint investment in common facilities and relocation, or to gather views on economic development policy; and
- mining companies and local residents meet to resolve conflicts.

Source: Asian Development Bank, derived from Law of Mongolia on Administrative and Territorial Units of Mongolia and Their Governance.

SUBNATIONAL GOVERNANCE AND SERVICE DELIVERY IN PRACTICE

This section explores how SNGs manage their primary levers of local public action, the delivery of the range of socioeconomic infrastructure and services for which they are responsible, and the constraints and issues that surround this.

A. Service Delivery Spending Responsibilities

1. Legal Mandates

Since 2012, there has been a degree of expenditure responsibility assigned to SNGs under the Budget Law (2012):

(i) Under Article 58, there is a set of modest, devolved service delivery functions of *aimags* and *soums*.

(ii) Under Articles 39.1 and 61.1, there is delegation of responsibilities for basic education, primary health care, social welfare, physical fitness, and culture to SNGs. These are funded through special-purpose fiscal transfers. In the most recent Budget Law revision, from 2019 some minor spending functions related to physical fitness, culture, and parts of school and clinic operating budgets will no longer be transferred to SNGs as devolved functions and funded from the base expenditure budget (Table 4).

However, these are recurrent budget responsibilities for which all local spending is subject to rigid central budget norms, greatly limiting any local choice.

Despite the provisions noted in Table 4, in practice, capital budget spending is still controlled by the central sector ministries. The main resource for local capital budget spending is the LDF transfer and for which there are menus for *aimags* and *soums*, although these are not always clear. For example, it is not clear if these menus are exclusive mandates for spending only to be undertaken by SNGs or permissive lists of allowable spending that the central government may decide to spend.

A review process of SNG functional assignments has been launched by the Cabinet Secretariat under the SDC-supported *Decentralisation Policy Support Program*. A methodology has been developed with initial piloting undertaken in the Ministry of Environment, which is now being extended to the Ministry of Construction and Urban Development and the Ministry of Labour. The next step will be to assess SNG capacity to adopt new functions.

Table 4: Functions Decentralized under the Budget Law

Sector	*Aimags* and Capital City	*Soums* and Districts
Main Functions Devolved (Budget Law, Article 58)		
Social Welfare	• Social care and welfare (upon a decision of SNG governors) • Playgrounds	• Social care and welfare (upon a decision of SNG governors) • Playgrounds
Transport, Roads	• Public transport • *Aimag* and Inter-*soum* roads • Street lighting	• Street lighting maintenance
Water and Sanitation	• Water supply • Sewerage, drainage • Waste removal • Public hygiene	• Public hygiene, street cleaning, waste removal
Agriculture and Livestock	• Livestock restocking • Pasture management • Pest control	• Livestock restocking • Pasture management
Economic Development	• O&M electric distribution network • Development of small and medium-sized enterprises	
Environment	• Environmental protection and rehabilitation • Flood protection	• Environmental protection
Capital Infrastructure	• Urban planning, construction of new infrastructure • Maintenance of locally owned buildings	
Main functions delegated (Budget Law, Articles 39.1 and 61.1)		
Education	• Preschool, general education, fitness, and culture	• Preschool, general education, fitness, and culture
Health	• Primary health care	• Primary health care
Social Welfare	• Child protection and development	• Child protection and development

O&M = operation and maintenance, SNG = subnational government.

Source: Asian Development Bank (compiled from the Budget Law of Mongolia, 2010).

The Cabinet Secretariat officially endorsed this methodology in a January 2018 circular to all ministries. The recent Budget Law revision included a provision under Article 58 that each ministry should review SNG assignments every 3 to 5 years. However, based on international experience, it remains to be seen how enthusiastically line ministries will move to cede to SNGs any control over their responsibilities and the associated budgetary and staff resources.

The Budget Law is not the only statute mandating functions to SNGs. Functions are scattered throughout other laws and regulations and not always aligned or updated and constitute a source of some confusion (Box 10).

Box 10: Unclear Mandates to Subnational Governments

In 2014, Ulaanbaatar City authorities undertook an extensive review of service delivery functions, roles, and procedures as laid down under the law. The findings were revealing.

(i) A large number of legal and regulatory instruments (137) in one way or another dictate service responsibilities to city authorities at one level or another.

(ii) A large number of service delivery responsibilities (536) are mandated to city, district, and *khoroo* (urban ward) authorities. For example:

- roads and related infrastructure maintenance: 34 responsibilities
- social policy: 75 responsibilities
- social protection and welfare: 122 responsibilities
- public order: 23 responsibilities
- environment: 29 responsibilities

(iii) A large degree of confusion existed across this range of responsibilities. Among the 536 distinct service responsibilities, there were 147 overlaps or conflicts in mandated responsibilities between city and districts, or districts and *khoroos*.

A similar review conducted by another *aimag* (province) counted 80 sector-specific laws or regulations that in different ways specify subnational government service delivery responsibilities.

Source: Consultations with Ulaanbaatar City officials.

2. Spending Patterns in Practice

Overall, subnational spending in 2017 constituted 26% of all national government spending, down from 29% in 2014 (Figure 3).

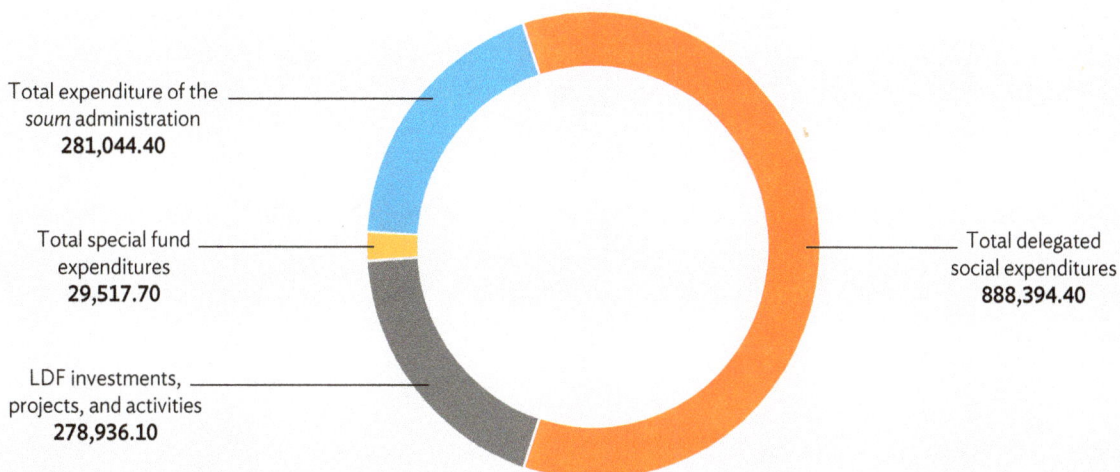

Figure 3: Expenditure Breakdown for Bayantal *Soum* (Govisumber), 2018
(MNT'000)

Total expenditure of the *soum* administration
281,044.40

Total special fund expenditures
29,517.70

LDF investments, projects, and activities
278,936.10

Total delegated social expenditures
888,394.40

LDF = Local Development Fund.
Source: Data provided by Bayantal *Soum* officials.

No national budget data on SNG spending by sector were available other than for Ulaanbaatar (Appendix 1). Based on field visits, it appears that the bulk of this spending is on the functions delegated to SNGs under Articles 39 and 61 (education, health, and social welfare), accounting for 60% of the budget. Most SNG revenues comprise transfers earmarked for these services.

National budget data are available on SNG spending by economic classification, revealing that on average, 80% of SNG spending is on current, mainly staff-related costs, with 20% on capital spending.[15]

3. Budget Expenditure Norms

In common with many other transition countries, budget spending under the decentralized functions outlined above is closely regulated by strict central budget expenditure norms, especially regarding recurrent budget spending, for both staff-related and other operation and maintenance costs. These are used to apply ex ante controls on SNG budgets.

These norms, which are issued as regulations jointly by the concerned sector ministry and by the MOF Expenditure Division, apply especially to recurrent spending on the delegated functions. They specify allowable rates for spending, for example, per pupil, per school, per square meter, or for books, meals, and heating. Spending on health care may be per patient or per facility, or for drugs, travel, heating, and water. These rates are applied to each *aimag*, and then by each *aimag* for each *soum* using official data on resident population, enrolled pupils, size of the facility, and so on.

There are similar Cabinet Secretariat and MOF norms for general spending by the SNG administration (Governor's Office, *hural*, etc.) that regulate allowable costs for offices, meetings, and travel, which are then allocated based on SNG populations and staff numbers. However, these norms have not been applied in the past 2 to 3 years because of the budget crisis. SNG budget proposals have simply been cut back across the board by MOF.

The purpose of such norms is to limit abuse by spending departments. Nevertheless, the evidence and discussions with SNG officials suggests these centrally issued budget norms may often undercut the legitimate role of SNGs, constitute a massive constraint on local decision-making flexibility, and interfere with efficient local public service delivery.

As illustrated in Box 11, they greatly limit the scope for local citizen engagement with SNGs since, all too often, these norms do not allow SNGs to respond flexibly to citizen needs. Similarly, they constrain the role of elected SNG *hurals* in providing input to SNG governors and departmental budget proposals or overseeing budget execution.

---

[15]   Analysis of data from the *National Statistical Yearbook of Mongolia* (2017).

Box 11: Issues Around Spending Responsibilities

The lack of clarity and ambivalence surrounding spending mandates, especially on the capital budget, makes it difficult (i) to determine the appropriate levels of subnational government (SNG) funding (e.g., through the Local Development Fund), and (ii) to hold SNGs accountable for the levels and quality of infrastructure and services. Functions are often vaguely described, different texts contradict each other, and the same function is assigned to more than one level or in some cases to the line ministry and in other cases to an SNG. This creates confusion at each SNG level regarding whether they or another SNG level or a sector department is responsible and discourages the mandates being taken as seriously as they should be. This lack of clarity greatly weakens the ability of citizens to lobby for better service delivery.

Even for decentralized functions, the rigid budget norms effectively deprive SNGs of discretionary powers needed to realize their potential comparative advantages that would allow them to tailor spending to their local context.

The functional assignment review exercise began with support from the Swiss Agency for Development and Cooperation and, embedded into policy, is a promising start. Without prejudging the outcomes, it appears that many functions are currently overcentralized. Both primary health and basic education are excellent candidates for devolved SNG management, but they have only been delegated to SNGs under arrangements that allow for minimal local discretion. Functional reassignment reforms will prove difficult to implement across sector ministries given the loss of central resource control that it will entail, at least without strong central political backing.

Source: Asian Development Bank (compiled based on consultations with government officials and representatives from development partners).

B. Financing Resources

1. Own-Source Revenues

■ Legal Revenue Powers

Under Article 23, the Budget Law assigns a set of modest tax and nontax revenues to SNGs while reducing the previous revenue-sharing between levels and assigning the bulk of mineral tax revenues to the central government (Table 5).

Paradoxically, this centralization of major revenue sources, while unpopular in those *aimags* where mining operations are located, is actually a reform that has paved the way for more equitable future decentralization of service functions since it has, potentially, allowed the central government the resources required for redistribution across the national territory through a future fiscal transfer mechanism.

The taxation rates for all such revenues, even if assigned to SNGs, are approved centrally by the MOF Revenue Division and the State *hural*, unless such powers have been delegated to SNG *hurals* as is the case for one or two land use-related fees.

All revenues are collected by the General Tax Department of MOF, which has offices in all SNGs.

Table 5: Decentralized Revenue Powers under the Budget Law

Aimags and Capital City	Soums and Districts
Tax Revenues, Fees and Charges (Budget Law Articles 23.6 and 23.8)	
• Personal income taxes (as under Article 8.1.1 of the pit law) • State stamp tax (other than that specified in Article 11.2 of State stamp tax law) • Capital city tax • Land fee • Immoveable property tax • Vehicle and carriage tax • Inheritance tax • 20% license fees for petroleum exploration and exploitation	• Personal income taxes (other than those collected by *aimags* and Capital City) • State stamp tax (other than that collected by *aimags* and the Capital City) • Hunting fees • License fees for natural resources other than mineral • Natural plant fees • Timber fees • Fee for the use of widespread mineral resources • Household water-use fee • Income tax of self-employed people • Dog fee • Waste removal charge • 10% license fee for petroleum exploration and exploitation
Other Revenues (Budget Law Articles 23.7 and 23.9)	
• Dividends on SNG-owned bodies • Charges and sales revenue from SNG-owned assets	• Dividends on SNG-owned bodies • Charges and sales revenue from SNG-owned assets

SNG = subnational government.
Source: Budget Law of Mongolia (2010).

■ Revenue Patterns in Practice

Based on the revenue powers in the Budget Law, the total tax and nontax revenues raised by all SNGs comprised 18% of all SNG revenues in 2017. The bulk of these stem from personal income taxes, with property revenues at a low 11%.

Most SNG revenues are generated in Ulaanbaatar, which accounted for over 60% of total SNG revenues that year (Figure 4). According to Ulaanbaatar officials, tax collection rates are much below their potential yield.

Figure 4: Breakdown of Own-Revenues of All Subnational Governments, 2017

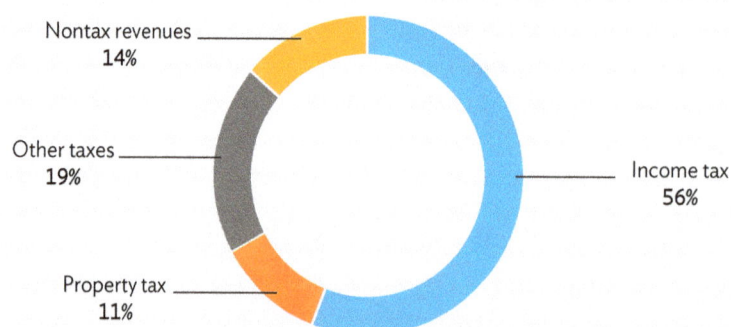

Nontax revenues 14%
Other taxes 19%
Property tax 11%
Income tax 56%

Source: Government of Mongolia. 2017. *National Statistical Yearbook.* Ulaanbaatar.

2. Fiscal Transfers

■ Overview

As almost everywhere in Asia, at least outside major metropolitan areas, SNGs are heavily reliant on fiscal transfers. Under the Budget Law, there are three main fiscal transfers to the SNGs: deficit transfers, special-purpose transfers, and local development fund transfers. Reflecting the inherited fiscal system, there are also fiscal transfers from SNGs upward to the central government from surplus SNGs, which in 2017 exceeded deficit transfers to SNGs.

Figure 5 summarizes the relative importance and trends in recent years (surplus transfers to the central government are denoted as negative SNG revenues). There is substantial evidence from other countries practicing similar surplus and/or deficit transfer mechanisms that they are replete with negative incentives for local revenue-raising and sound local planning and budgeting.

Figure 5: **Fiscal Transfers to and from Subnational Governments (MNT million)**

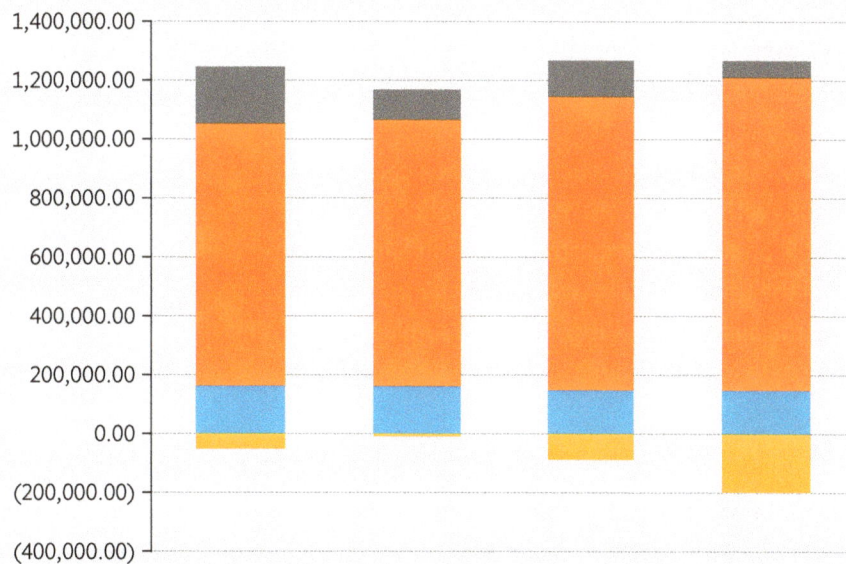

	2014	2015	2016	2017 (est.)
■ Surplus transfers to central government	(52,750.40)	(12,989.20)	(90,681.20)	(195,414.80)
■ LDF transfers	195,387.00	105,984.80	120,267.70	53,013.50
■ Special-purpose transfers	892,304.40	904,380.20	995,259.30	1,066,608.30
■ Deficit transfers	158,138.90	160,494.00	150,987.30	146,162.10

( ) = negative, LDF = Local Development Fund, MNT = Mongolian togrog.

Source: Government of Mongolia. 2017. *National Statistical Yearbook*. Ulaanbaatar.

Upward Transfers from Surplus Subnational Governments to Central Government

Based on Article 56.2 of the Budget Law and reflecting the public finance paradigm that Mongolia has inherited, revenue-surplus SNGs must share upward to the central government a part of their surplus where approved base revenue exceeds base expenditure. Aside from Ulaanbaatar, which has a revenue base far greater than other *aimags*, surplus SNGs are those benefiting from mineral or petroleum revenues (Table 6).

Legally mandated sharing arrangements have been changing in recent years, with a substantial increase in the upward sharing rate in the 3 years since the budget crisis. Increased SNG retention of surpluses is now planned to start from 2019.

In 2017, upward sharing was 17% of all SNG own-revenues. For surplus SNGs (Ulaanbaatar and six *aimags* in 2017), this sometimes represented a much greater share of their own-revenues (Table 7).

Similarly, surplus *soums* must also share a part of their revenues with respective *aimags*. No national data are available on this, but to illustrate, mission findings found that of the three *soums* in Govisumber *aimag*, Sumber *soum*, the *aimag* center, is generally in surplus. Of the nine Ulaanbaatar districts, three are generally in surplus.

Table 6: Changes in Upward Sharing Rates for Surplus Revenues

Fiscal Year	Share of Surplus Transferred Upward (%)
2016	30
2017	40
2018	60
2019	40
2020	30

Source: Compiled from Ministry of Finance data.

Table 7: Share of Own-Revenues Sent to Central Government by Surplus Subnational Governments, 2017

Aimag	Share (%)
Bulgan	1
Orkhon	27
Govisumber	2
Darkhan-Uul	1
Dornogovi	2
Umnugovi	25
Ulaanbaatar	21

Source: Government of Mongolia. 2017. *National Statistical Yearbook.* Ulaanbaatar.

Deficit Transfers

These are transfers made to SNGs at *aimag* or *soum* level to cover the deficit between approved base expenditures and revenues under Articles 56.1 and 56.4 of the Budget Law and reflect inherited public finance traditions. It should be emphasized that these transfers are not grants in the usual sense but are determined after SNGs have submitted their budget proposals to the central government and serve as a mechanism to address the gap between estimated SNG revenues and expenditures.

In 2017, 15 *aimags* received such transfers. These transfers constituted 6% of all SNG revenues and accounted for 13% of all SNG's own-revenues.

However, for individual deficit SNGs, they were in some cases significant. For Khuvsgul, 21% and for Uvs 20% of all revenues, which amounted to 134% for Khuvsgul and 154% for Uvs' own-revenues.

■ Special-Purpose Transfers

These are transfers to the SNGs under Article 61.2 of the Budget Law to finance recurrent expenditures for the functions delegated to SNGs under Articles 39.1 and 61.1, and which had, until 2012, been on central government budgets. These were preschool, general education, cultural services, primary health care, land and cadaster services, child development and protection, and public fitness activities. Their allocation is based on agreements negotiated between individual *aimags* and the sector ministries concerned, and between *soums* and their *aimags*.

These special-purpose transfers are not grants in the usual sense, i.e., they are not pre-allocated to SNGs in the way that LDF grants are. They are instead funding windows to which SNGs apply and from which allocations are then made centrally by the sector ministry and by MOF. The actual allocations for SNG expenditures for these delegated functions are made in reference to prior contractual agreements, themselves tightly determined by sets of budget norms which dictate all staff-related and other operating costs, and which leave SNGs almost no discretion. It may be that other considerations shape the central allocations of these transfers as well, otherwise, it is difficult to explain the per capita variance noted below.

Table 8 shows the breakdown for transfers for education and health ministries and functions for 2018, where preschools and secondary schools account for 90%.

These combined transfers constitute the bulk of all transfers (in 2017, 44% of all SNG revenues, ranging from 30% of Ulaanbaatar revenues to 79% of Govisumber revenues).

Since 2019, through a recent revision to the Budget Law, cultural services and fitness activities have been transferred as SNG-devolved functions to be included in base expenditures and hence financed by own-revenues and deficit transfers. Special-purpose transfers have accordingly been reduced from seven to five. Since neither of these two functions entail major spending, it is unlikely they will result in any great reduction of the total special-purpose transfers.

Table 8: Deficit Transfers as a Share of Subnational Government Revenues (%)

	All Revenues (including transfers)	Own-Revenues Only
Bayan-Ulgii	17	136
Govi-Altai	37	165
Zavkhan	17	99
Uvs	20	154
Khovd	14	83
Arkhangai	19	101
Bayankhongor	18	91
Bulgan	0	0
Orkhon	0	0
Uvurkhangai	17	87
Khuvsgul	21	134
Govisumber	0	0
Darkhan-Uul	0	0
Dornogovi	0	0
Dundgovi	16	84
Umnugovi	0	0
Selenge	5	16
Tuv	12	49
Dornod	6	16
Sukhbaatar	12	49
Khentii	16	78
Ulaanbaatar	0	0

Source: Government of Mongolia. 2017. *National Statistical Yearbook.* Ulaanbaatar.

These transfers are approved by the central government and the State *hural* on an *aimag* basis. Each *aimag* then allocates to its constituent *soums* (see Recurrent Budgeting section).

However, there is reason to believe that for *aimag*-center *soums*, no such allocations are made, presumably because the expenditures in those urban areas are retained under *aimag* authority. This is suggested by the revenue budget for Sumber *soum*, which shows a zero entry for these transfers (Table 9). If so, this appears to be another example of the unclarity in mandates for SNG tiers or the excessive discretion left to *aimags* regarding resource allocation across *soums*.

Table 9: Sumber *Soum* Revenue Budget, 2018

Main Special-Purpose Transfers	
Ministry/Function	MNT (million)
Ministry of Education	**988,529.40**
• Preschool	311,267.40
• Secondary Schools	619,370.00
• Culture	45,245.00
• Fitness and Sports	12,647.00
Ministry of Health	**113,313.10**

Source: Consultations with Sumber *Soum* officials.

■ Local Development Fund Transfers

These are transfers to the SNGs under Article 60 of the Budget Law. They are essentially the only budget resources available to SNGs for discretionary capital investment spending. The LDF transfer mechanism comprises two components: a formula-based grant component and a revenue-sharing by derivation component (Box 12).

Planning and management of the LDF by SNGs are guided by a Ministry of Finance LDF regulation recently revised with support from the SLP3. The SLP3 is also developing a capacity support program for SNGs.

The introduction of the LDF as a budgetary resource allowing genuine local priority-setting for the first time has sparked considerable interest within local civil society groups eager to engage with SNGs and among development partners. Several projects aim to build capacity around this mechanism.

The overall LDF transfer flows from both components since the mechanism was introduced show a sharp decline from 2015 as the budget crisis emerged and as changes to the allocation mechanism were introduced. In 2014, LDF transfers represented 16% of all transfers and 5% of all SNG revenues. By 2017, the corresponding shares were only 4% for transfers and 1% for SNG revenues. The relative importance of LDF transfers for SNGs other than Ulaanbaatar remains much greater (Figure 6).

Box 12: **Components of the Local Development Fund Funding Mechanism**

The General Local Development Fund: Formula-Based

The General Local Development Fund (GLDF) is a national pool established under Article 59, from various national revenue sources, currently at 5% from value-added tax, and 30% from petroleum royalties. These sources and funding rates have changed over time. For example, for some years, sources included a share of the upward-shared revenues from surplus subnational governments (SNGs). Annual allocations are made from this pool to *aimags* according to a formula based on four criteria:

(i)   *aimag* development index (a composite socioeconomic index compiled by the National Development Agency);

(ii) *aimag* population;

(iii) population density, remoteness, and size of territory; and

(iv) *aimag* tax initiatives.

An additional portion of the national GLDF pool is funded from 5% of the mineral exploitation tax revenues. This is allocated to *aimags* on a per capita formula basis but with a preferential increase of up to 10% for those areas where these revenues were generated.

Each *aimag*, in turn, allocates a share of its GLDF transfers to its *soums*. This sharing arrangement has been altered in two ways since 2017 as part of the government's attempt to manage the budget crisis induced by the severe drop in mining revenues:

(i)   The *aimag* LDF pool was partly earmarked for certain base expenditures, reducing substantially the part that could be used for discretionary investment spending by *aimags* or which could be reallocated to *soums*.

(ii) The share of this net *aimag* LDF pool to be allocated to *soums* was also reduced from 70% to 40%.

Revenue-Sharing by Derivation: Earmarked for the Local Development Fund

Provisions have been introduced into the Budget Law in recent years under Articles 60.6 and 60.7, whereby a portion of the revenues from mining royalties and exploration fees are to be shared with the areas of revenue collection for LDF spending. This provision was first applied in 2016 but was suspended during the budget crisis period and then reintroduced in 2019.

Source: Asian Development Bank (compiled from consultations with Ministry of Finance officials).

Figure 6: **Trends in Local Development Fund Transfers to Subnational Governments**

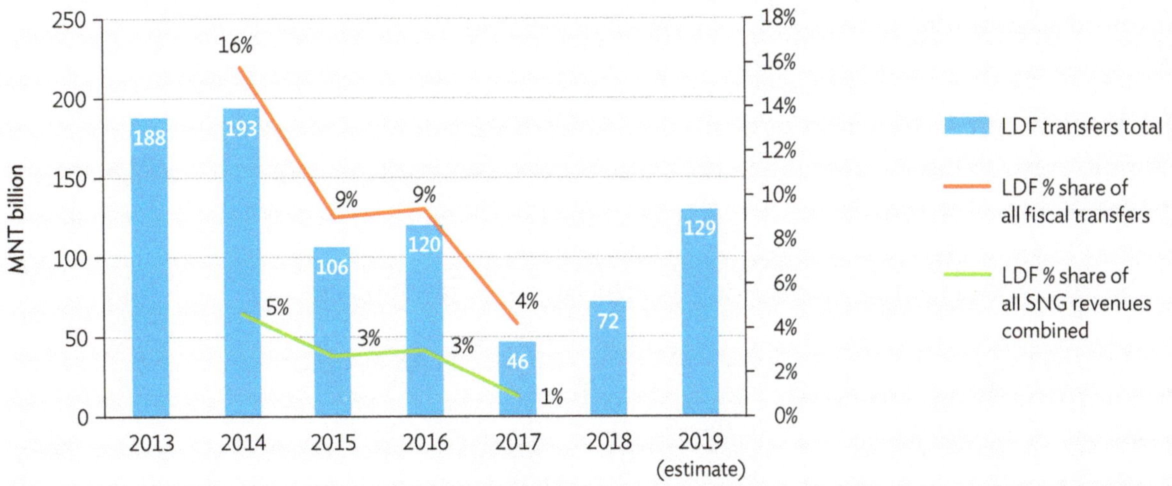

LDF = Local Development Fund, MNT = Mongolian togrog, SNG = subnational government.
Sources: Government of Mongolia. 2017. *National Statistical Yearbook.* Ulaanbaatar; budget projections from the Ministry of Finance.

Some additional funding for the LDF mechanism (totaling approximately $20 million or MNT8 billion over the period 2017–2020) is provided by the World Bank under the SLP3 project (Appendix 2).

This recent decline has been especially severe at *soum* level given the netting-out of certain base expenditures from the *aimag* LDF pools and the dramatic reduction in *aimag*-to-*soum* sharing ratio noted above.

■ Revenue-Sharing by Derivation

When a portion of revenues assigned to the central government is returned to or allowed to be retained by the SNGs where they were collected, this constitutes a fiscal transfer. The Budget Law provides for certain mining-related revenues to be so shared but earmarked for the SNG LDF account. This sharing was suspended but restarted in 2019.

Since 2019, 50% of the air pollution fee on brown coal will be returned to SNGs for general budget use.

Many officials view such revenue-sharing as "giving back" revenue powers rather than a central transfer. This perspective is not surprising since SNGs have little real tax power over rate decisions, even over those sources formally assigned to them.

■ Other Fiscal Transfers

The government committed to providing a temporary, targeted investment fund transfer to *aimags* over the 2-year period preceding the 2020 elections. This amounted to MNT59 billion in 2018 and MNT189 billion in 2019. Added to the LDF, these transfers will more than double the discretionary investment resources of SNGs over this period. However, it is unclear how they will be managed. Since there is no provision in the Budget Law, they are not subject to the revised LDF regulation, and no specific guidance has been provided. This is not considered a major issue since all indications are this is a one-off resource transfer introduced for political reasons.

Other, more modest transfers have been or are being provided to SNGs, for example, the *soum* Development Fund (loans to *soums* from the former Ministry of Economic Development), transfers to promote small and medium-sized enterprises, transfers for livestock, and for environmental protection. No national budget data was available for such transfers, but in one *soum,* the livestock protection and *soum* development funds together constituted 2% of all *soum* revenues compared to 60% from special-purpose transfers and 19% from the LDF.

3. Subnational Government Resources and Equity Patterns

All the budget resources outlined on a per capita basis per *aimag* are depicted in Table 10 and Figure 7.

Own-revenues are not distributed evenly on a per capita basis. Ulaanbaatar and the *aimags* hosting mining operations both enjoy high levels of revenue. Similarly, deficit transfers are distributed according to the budget surplus and deficit logic that prevails.

Table 10: *Aimag* **Budget Resources per Capita, 2017 (variance)**

	FISCAL RESOURCES: MNT PER CAPITA – 2017				
	Deficit Transfers	Own-Source Revenue	Special-Purpose Transfers	LDF	Total Revenue
Bayan-Ulgii	119,157	87,748	482,549	16,283	705,737
Govi-Altai	158,142	95,747	138,236	38,066	430,190
Zavkhan	147,109	149,218	522,276	23,699	842,302
Uvs	149,869	97,584	489,924	20,700	758,077
Khovd	100,008	119,986	460,691	20,347	701,032
Arkhangai	133,895	132,441	410,680	20,940	697,957
Bayankhongor	140,498	154,905	442,975	24,808	763,186
Bulgan	–	369,770	476,151	28,144	874,065
Orkhon	–	495,974	328,227	19,089	843,290
Uvurkhangai	107,310	123,612	391,011	19,480	641,413
Khuvsgul	140,912	105,202	424,178	16,551	686,843
Govisumber	–	432,673	1,915,064	67,706	2,415,443
Darkhan-Uul	–	212,750	332,646	17,402	562,799
Dornogovi	–	366,768	425,280	33,827	825,875
Dundgovi	135,616	160,784	511,210	39,801	847,411
Umnugovi	–	1,771,289	431,941	48,633	2,251,862
Selenge	35,377	218,868	428,642	19,666	702,554
Tuv	93,191	189,343	452,546	19,134	754,215
Dornod	40,111	246,935	379,402	26,215	692,664
Sukhbaatar	94,871	195,531	468,103	25,364	783,868
Khentii	122,515	156,233	450,673	26,255	755,676
Ulaanbaatar	–	515,665	224,843	8,341	748,849
Mean	78,117	290,865	481,239	26,384	876,605
Median	97,440	175,064	437,458	22,319	754,945
Max	158,142	1,771,289	1,915,064	67,706	2,415,443
Min	–	87,748	138,236	8,341	430,190
Max:Min ratio	NA	20.2	13.9	8.1	5.6

– = data on means not available, LDF = Local Development Fund, MNT = Mongolian togrog, NA = not applicable.

Note: Cells in darker shade are values above the mean; cells in lighter shade are below the mean.

Source: Government of Mongolia. 2017. *National Statistical Yearbook*. Ulaanbaatar.

Figure 7: **Revenues per Capita of Subnational Governments by Source and Variance, 2017**

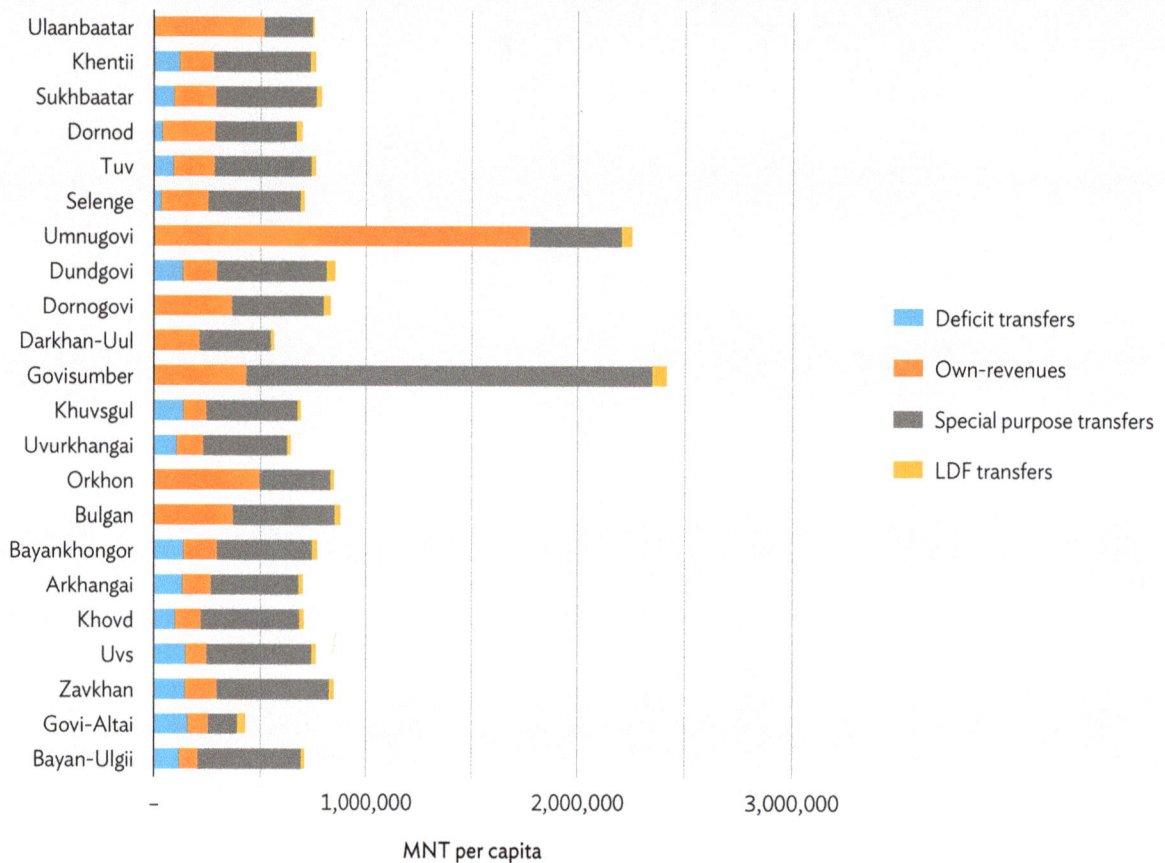

LDF = Local Development Fund, MNT = Mongolian togrog.

Source: Analysis of data from Government of Mongolia. 2017. *National Statistical Yearbook.* Ulaanbaatar.

What is striking is the large variance in fiscal transfers per capita, notably the special-purpose transfers, for which the max:min ratio is around 14:1. This is largely due to the high special transfer allocations to Umnugovi and Govisumber, the reasons for which are unclear. If these are removed, the variance between other *aimags* is much lower. No national data are available on *soum* revenues per capita, but there is reason to believe the variance at *soum* level is much greater. The LDF variance is also significant, although lower, with a max:min ratio of 8:1. For 2017, given the suspension of the revenue-sharing provision, there were only formula-based General Local Development Fund allocations.

There appears to be similar variance and inequity in per capita spending patterns across the districts within Ulaanbaatar (Appendix 1).[16] There is no reason budget resources per capita should be equal across SNGs since need and cost factors may vary considerably. Nonetheless, it is difficult to see how such wide variances around the mean can be justified and the issue warrants review (Box 13).

---

[16]   World Bank. 2017. *Toward Inclusive Service Delivery in Ulaanbaatar, Mongolia.* Washington, DC.

Box 13: **Issues Arising from Subnational Government Financing**

Own Revenue Assignments

The revenue sources assigned are relatively modest and powers to change tax rates on these sources are almost all centralized. However, it is reported that even this potential is not fully exploited and fiscal effort is low. This may be due to weak local capacities in maintaining databases, making assessments, and administering collection, and weak incentives for local fiscal effort embedded in the inherited surplus and deficit paradigm.

Fiscal Transfer Arrangements

- Although the government has now been able to establish fiscal transfer mechanisms, having recentralized many important revenue powers, there are still potentially serious horizontal equity issues across *aimags* (provinces). The two major instruments (fiscal transfers and own revenue assignments) need to be explored in light of real spending-need variations.
- There is no readily available national data on fiscal transfers to *soums*, which is worrying. The partial evidence on Local Development Fund transfers to *soums* suggests there may be even greater horizontal inequities at that level.
- Whether the Local Development Fund transfers are sufficient to address the vertical gap is hard to assess given the unclear capital spending responsibilities of subnational government (SNGs). As for special-purpose transfers in the social sectors, these responsibilities appear not to be properly costed, and thus, by default, reliance is on older, standard budget norms.
- There is still a strong belief rooted in politics and history that mining and other natural resource-revenues belong to local authorities, and it is "proper" to return them, at least in part. However, there is no clarity on the policy rationale for such sharing. For example, at times officials refer to the need for SNGs to enjoy extra resources to address social and environmental costs of mining and other times to their right to retain such revenues.

General

There is no central monitoring of overall SNG revenue patterns even at the *aimag* level, either within the Ministry of Finance or in the central government, and there is no information on *soum* revenue patterns.

Source: Asian Development Bank (compiled from consultations with Ministry of Finance and local government officials).

C. Planning, Budgeting, and Delivery Procedures

1. Strategic and Medium-Term Planning

The Development Policy Planning Law (2016) aims to provide a consistent framework for national, sector, and regional planning to ensure a link between short-term and more strategic long-term planning and to empower the national planning agency (previously the Ministry of Economic Development, and now the NDA) with a stronger interministerial coordinating role. It also mandates public consultation at key stages. Various planning exercises are undertaken relating to the subnational level.

■ Regional and Sector Plans

(i)   The NDA prepares regional development plans for clusters of *aimags*.

(ii)   The major sector ministries undertake long- and medium-term plans for education, health, and other services that have a geographic or regional dimension.

■ Spatial and Master Plans for Urban Centers

(i)   Ulaanbaatar has prepared a master plan for 2020–2040 through the Urban Planning, Architecture, and Design Institute and Master Planning Agency of Capital City. These are both deconcentrated agencies of the Ministry of Construction and Urban Development. The master plan must be approved by the State *hural* after Ulaanbaatar *hural* approval.

(ii)   Other cities, such as Darkhan, hire consultants to develop master plans under supervision by the Ministry of Construction and Urban Development.

■ Governor Action Plans

More important from an operational standpoint, all incoming SNG governors prepare an action plan for their 4-year mandate, which is submitted for *hural* approval. These plans are driven in part by the national or local policy agendas of the local majority party but shaped by local priorities. If SNGs are to have any role in shaping their budgets, these action plans are key (Box 14).

Box 14: The Practice of Development Planning

To date, the Development Policy Planning Law (2016) appears to have had little impact. There seems to be little coordination between sector planning and urban master planning. For example, Ulaanbaatar authorities see little consultation with sector ministries. The same is true for ministry consultations with the less prominent *aimag* and *soum* authorities. Implementation of the public consultation provisions by the subnational governments (SNGs) is undermined by the uncertainties in the capital budget, except for allocations from the Local Development Fund.

Urban master plans appear to be conducted by consultants for the SNGs or the Ministry of Construction and Urban Development. These are often inspired by model urban templates from elsewhere and with a wish list of investments attached.

Generally, most master planning exercises remain on paper as aspirations but are unconnected to budget spending. Their main value is the part devoted to land-use zoning within urban areas, insofar as SNG authorities have any powers to regulate and enforce such regulations.

It is unclear how the four-yearly SNG Governor's Action Plans are formulated and how consistency is achieved across *aimags* (provinces) and *soums* (districts). These plans can only hope to influence the allocation of the relatively modest Local Development Fund.

Source: Asian Development Bank (compiled from consultations with local government officials).

---

2. Annual Planning and Budgeting Preparation and Execution

This section examines the process for shaping public spending, service delivery, and quality levels. The annual SNG planning, budgeting, and PFM procedures are regulated by the Budget Law and by various MOF regulations on budget preparation, budget execution, internal controls, reporting, asset management, treasury, and the LDF. Procurement is governed by the Public Procurement Law. In addition, there are sets of budget norms issued by education, health, and other sector ministries that govern the budget preparation process for the delegated functions financed by special-purpose transfers and by the Cabinet Secretariat for the general SNG administration budget (Box 15).

Box 15: **Actors in the Budget Process**

Article 4.1.36: General Budget Governor: SNG governors are "authorized to plan budgets for the area within their authority and allocate, oversee, manage, and report on the execution of the approved budgets in accordance with legislation."

Article 4.1.38: Direct Budget Governors: Heads of SNG sector departments and budget units such as schools, clinics are "authorized to plan budget resources for functions assigned by a general budget governor or central budget governor and manage the budget resources and report on its execution in accordance with legislation."

Source: Budget Law of Mongolia (2010).

◼ Recurrent Budgeting

Steps and Timetable

The annual budget timetable is set out in the Budget Law and regulations as depicted in Box 16.

Box 16: **Steps and Timetable for the Recurrent Budget Process**

1. By 15 June, the general and direct budget governors at the *soum* (district) level (the *soum* governors, the heads of budget entities such as schools, and heads of sector departments) compile their revenue estimates and expenditure budget proposals separately and send them in parallel to the *aimag* (province).

    - Until 2018, these proposals were sent to their corresponding *aimag* departments (sector departments or *aimag* Governor's Office), where they were reviewed and adjusted. These were then submitted separately to the Cabinet Secretariat and sector ministries for further review and adjustment and then to the Ministry of Finance (MOF).
    - From 2019, there has been a change in regard to proposals for spending on utilities (power, heat, water), in which *soum* or *aimag* sector departments and budget units now submit through the *aimag* Governor's Office for review, and then directly to the MOF, thus bypassing central sector ministries. All budget proposals for staff-related spending and consumables will continue to go to sector ministries as before.

2. By 5 July, *aimag* governors are notified of ceilings for base expenditures for devolved functions within the Medium-Term Fiscal Framework for the following year, excluding delegated social sector spending.

3. By 15 August, the general and direct budget governors at the *aimag* level compile their proposals, including those they have accepted from the *soums*, then submit sector proposals to sector ministries along with SNG governors' proposals to the Cabinet Secretariat.

4. Between mid-August and end-September, sector ministries and the Cabinet Secretariat review all proposals in view of the various budget norms and other policy considerations, make adjustments, and then submit proposals to the MOF.

5. From early September to 5 October, MOF reviews revenue estimates and expenditure proposals against the various budget norms and final adjustments are made with approved revenue and expenditure levels for each *aimag* and its deficit or surplus status.

6. By 5 October, MOF submits the combined budget proposal to the State *hural*.

7. By 15 November, the State *hural* approves the final state budget after review of the budget proposal and a series of consultations with MOF officials in committees and then in plenary. This budget indicates approved overall central government and *aimag* budgets, which include but do not specify the budget allocations for *soums*, and also deficit and other transfers to *aimags*.

continued on next page

Box 16: *Continued*

8. By the second half of November, MOF communicates these approved budgets to the *aimags*. Each *aimag* must then finalize its own budget within the given budget ceilings and determine budget allocations and transfers for its *soums*. The *aimag* budget is then submitted to the *aimag hural* (elected assembly) by the end of November. In this process, the *aimag* enjoys some measure of discretion since, for example, the approved education budget for different categories of school spending is not earmarked by the school. Hence, the *aimag* has some latitude in allocating special-purpose transfers between budget units (kindergartens, schools, dormitories, clinics, etc.) across *soums* as it sees fit.

9. By the end of November, *aimags* inform the *soums* of their budgets, and thereafter, each *soum* must finalize and approve its budget and submit it to the *soum hural* for approval by 15 December. Final *soum* budgets are then shared with the *aimag* but not with the MOF.

Sources: Interviews with MOF and local officials and author's analysis of provisions in the Budget Law.

Although *aimags* are notified of budget ceilings determined by the Medium-Term Fiscal Framework before submitting their base spending proposals, these limits are often not respected in the proposals. *Aimags* do not generally transmit any ceilings to the *soums*. Final approved current budgets are usually much less than the original proposals. While salary-related budgets are more or less approved as submitted, cuts are made, especially to nonsalary operating costs (consumables, fuel, and other travel costs, office equipment and stationery, etc.), which tend to be maintained at previous levels (Box 17).

Budgeting can cause serious problems for SNG functioning. In Bayangaal *soum,* the norm-based travel budget approved for the *soum* administration was MNT405,000 per month, but actual expenses incurred averaged MNT900,000 monthly. In one example, the *soum* administration incurred an outstanding debt with a fuel supplier and then, arguing the case as a fait accompli, relied on payment by the *aimag* Governor's Office at the end of the year from the *aimag* reserve fund.

MOF receives no reports on *aimag-soum* allocations or *soum* budgets and so cannot monitor the PFM at this level across *aimags*.

■ Capital Investment Budgeting

The Budget Law mandates planning, construction, and maintenance of capital infrastructure assets as an SNG responsibility. This is not another sector but refers to assets (nurseries, schools, clinics, heating plants, sewerage pipes and tanks, water points and networks, etc.), which, alongside staff and other recurrent inputs, are essential to delivering basic services such as water, sewerage, public lighting, irrigation, heating, education, and health. Here we must distinguish between SNG planning and budgeting for the LDF and other SNG sector capital budgeting.

Local Development Fund

The funding and allocation arrangements for the LDF were detailed earlier. The procedures and timetable for the LDF planning and management cycle are detailed in Table 11.

Box 17: Issues Arising from Recurrent Budgeting Process

Despite announcements to *aimags* (provinces) about budget ceilings in the Medium-Term Fiscal Framework, these ceilings relate to base expenditures for devolved responsibilities but do not cover delegated social sector spending, which is a large portion of the total subnational government (SNG) spending. Often, the ceilings are not respected in the proposals submitted by *aimags*. *Aimags* generally do not inform the *soums* (districts) about ceilings that would guide their budget proposals.

Consequently, both *soums* and *aimags* continue to bid for funding with inflated budget proposals, especially for nonstaff recurrent costs that may not be subject to budget norms.

Similarly, there is no clear guidance on budget priorities by sector in a way that would translate sector policies into spending priorities. By default, priorities are given to salary costs determined by the staff establishment status quo, while other vital operating and maintenance activities are funded only as a residual. This is likely to compromise the quality of health and education services, where quality is so dependent on these other inputs.

The inevitable cutting back of proposals to what is affordable is done at the central level in the sector ministries and Ministry of Finance on the basis of standard budget norms. Even without such norms, there is no room or scope to weigh the merits and trade-offs of varying allocations across *aimags*, let alone across *soums*, given the lack of time or opportunity for consultation with local officials.

Budget norms are unnecessarily rigid and have probably not been adjusted for inflation. Similarly, they are applied in reference to population and other data, which are usually out of date, especially in fast growing cities like Ulaanbaatar, nor do they take into account the use of services offered in one area by residents of another. For example, Govisumber claims that its school and health facilities are used by residents of up to 10 *soums* in neighboring *aimags*.

Subnational governments regularly use supplier credit arrangements, especially with publicly-owned local utility budget units as a tactic to address their budget shortfalls in hopes of pressuring governors to cover the liability by year-end from reserve funds. This may seem pragmatic, but the practice is open to abuse.

These arrangements leave considerable discretion to the *aimags* in regard to the size and composition of *soum* budgets. It is not fully clear how this is done or what guidance is given. In Govisumber, there is an *aimag* governor's resolution that makes special-purpose transfer allocations on some population-based criteria, but there is ample room for error, patronage, and inequity.

The final budget approval process by local *hurals* (elected assemblies), especially at the *soum* level, is largely a rubber-stamp exercise since the elements of the budget have been largely fixed. All that remains open for debate is the Local Development Fund.

Source: Asian Development Bank (based on consultations with local government officials).

Since 2013, the LDF has been implemented with no operational guidelines to help SNGs manage the process other than MOF LDF Regulations 244 and 43. Many practices have been observed and there are concerns about mismanagement. With SLP3 support, MOF has revised the LDF regulation and is developing operational guidelines for SNGs to address these issues.

There are no available national budget data on sectoral breakdowns of LDF investments, although the MOF's LDF management information system potentially allows this to be generated, but they comprise a wide range: water supplies, roads and bridges, parks, and playgrounds, street lighting, public toilets and showers, equipping nurseries, schools, and clinics. All SNGs put aside an amount from the LDF for the annual Nadaam festival in July. Typically, *soums* allocate a standard MNT5 million.

Table 11: Local Development Fund Planning and Budgeting Timetable

Timing	Step
1st Quarter FY N-1	Polling or questionnaires to households
2nd Quarter FY N-1	*Bagh* (rural ward) or *khoroo* (urban ward) meetings to vote on priorities
3rd Quarter FY N-1	*Soum* (district) or district governor's working group vets, appraises, prioritizes
3rd Quarter FY N-1	Priority proposals submitted to governor
3rd Quarter FY N-1	Governor submits priority proposals to *soum* or district *hural* or refers up to *aimag* (province) governor
End November FY N-1	Ministry of Finance informs *aimag*/Ulaanbaatar of LDF allocations, which inform *soum* or district of their LDF allocations
Mid-December FY N-1	*Aimag*/Ulaanbaatar *hurals* and *soum* or district *hural* select and approve priority projects within annual budget
End December FY N-1	*Soum* informs *aimag* or Ulaanbaatar and budgets ratified
From January/February FY-N	LDF funds allocated in tranches by the Ministry of Finance through *aimag* or *soum* treasuries for budget execution

FY = fiscal year, FY N-1 = FY preceding the FY in which the allocation of LDF funds takes place, LDF = Local Development Fund.
Source: Consultations with Ministry of Finance officials.

Under the SLP3, MOF is piloting an annual performance assessment for all 330 *soums* with field surveys outsourced to independent contractors. The top performers receive a top-up of 25% of their basic allocation as an incentive. This appears to work well, but questions remain as to how this can be institutionalized after the project ends and whether it can be extended to *aimags*.

Other Capital Budgeting

Generally, SNGs have no capital budget resources other than the LDF. In certain cases, the few surplus SNGs may use a portion of their surplus for investments. Consequently, SNG sector departments and SNG governors submit capital spending proposals upward, often as parallel, uncoordinated requests, along a similar path and timetable as the recurrent budget proposals to their respective sector ministry, the Cabinet Secretariat, or the DLA. These bodies review the proposals in the light of sector submission to the State *hural* for final approval. For 2018, Govisumber *aimag* submitted investment proposals for MNT30 billion, of which only MNT2 billion was approved.

■ Budget Execution and Asset Management

General Treasury Issues

Since Mongolia operates a single treasury system, SNG budget execution is affected by chronic treasury problems stemming from general revenue shortfalls or overestimates, resulting in reduced or delayed transfers. This problem affects SNG revenues even more, since these are often more cyclical than those of the central government. Paradoxically, surplus *aimags or soums* may therefore be more vulnerable to seasonal revenue shortfalls than others.

In some cases, *soums* facing such problems may be granted a short-term overdraft credit facility by their *aimags*. In 2018, Sumber *soum* (a surplus *soum*) was accorded such a credit by Govisumber *aimag* amounting to MNT774 million. This was 44% of the overall *soum* budget to be repaid within the year.

These shortfall issues are seen under more discretionary budget headings and particularly for mechanisms such as the LDF, where such delays and midyear cutbacks have been frequent. These problems inevitably affect the level and quality of investment and service delivery.

Conversely, for certain categories such as the LDF, budget savings can be carried over to the next year. These are often unspent funds that may have been transferred too late in the year or in the winter season when procurement is difficult (Box 18).

Box 18: Issues Arising from the Local Development Fund and Other Capital Planning and Budgeting

Local Development Fund Planning and Budgeting

There is a lack of clarity around the eligible menu or what is allowed and excluded, in the respective menus of *soums* (districts) and *aimags* (provinces), especially in regard to recurrent costs, and whether these are exclusive mandates or merely permissible expenditures.

The varying financing arrangements for the General Local Development Fund (LDF) pool, which together with the cyclical nature of certain revenues, has made this an unpredictable resource for subnational governments (SNGs) from year to year and within the year, with actual LDF transfers often being less than the approved budget for that year.

The significant horizontal inequity inherent in the reintroduction of sharing certain mining revenues by derivation.

The discretion given to *aimags* in determining onward allocations to *soums*, mirroring the same discretion enjoyed for the recurrent budget.

There are incentives to submit undercosted investment proposals so that once approved and underway, it becomes easier to gain approval for funding cost overruns in the next budget year.

There is a lack of guidance on planning and management of the LDF and a mechanical bias in selecting investments based solely on citizen votes regardless of other development considerations or likely benefits and costs. This partly reflects the heritage of the LDF, widely seen as a community investment fund rather than a broad capital investment transfer to SNGs.

General Capital Budgeting

There is a lack of clarity about SNG spending mandates on the investment budget as defined in the Budget Law.

The August budget circular to *aimags* includes capital budget ceilings for the next year for devolved base spending, but these ceilings do not appear to be respected in the proposals made to the central government. The ceilings are not communicated to *soums*, and there are no advance ceilings for SNG capital spending in the important delegated social sectors. This encourages inflated proposals from which selections for approval are made centrally, not locally.

The potential added-value of SNGs in better understanding how to weigh local needs and priorities and ensuring intersectoral coordination is lost in the silo-based channeling of proposals to Ulaanbaatar, with little or no intersectoral scrutiny. The local *hural* (elected assembly) is absent in this process. This can mean, for example, that important local trade-off considerations are neglected, considering that SNGs are best placed to assess between investment expenditure proposals across water systems, schools, or clinics within the same SNG jurisdiction.

Despite the general provisions in the Development Policy Planning Law, there has been little practical guidance in regard to investment appraisal and prioritization, whether this is done intra- or intersectorally. Apparently, such procedures are now being introduced.

continued on next page

Box 18: *Continued*

SNGs generally express frustration that they do not know why certain proposals are not approved, and feel discouraged by the lack of consultation and clear criteria in this process. For 2018, Govisumber *Aimag* submitted proposals for MNT30 billion, of which only MNT2 billion were approved. *Aimag* officials were unclear as to the rationale for the approvals.

As with LDF planning, there seems to be an incentive to submit undercosted investment proposals so that once underway it is easier to get approval for funding cost overruns in the next budget year.

There is little clarity around the respective capital budget mandates of *soums* and *aimags*, with the distinction apparently coming down to investment size.

The Development Policy Planning Law would allow *soums* and *aimags* to procure and implement certain small or medium projects, even when on the central budget, but this is often denied to them. For SNGs, this can cause frustration, especially given that they believe they are better able to select and manage contractors in situ.

Lastly, in contrast to recurrent budget spending, decisions on more visible investment proposals often attract a lot of interest and involvement, especially from national Members of Parliament. Ulaanbaatar officials reported that their proposals for school investments in different *gers* (portable, sturdy tents) were sometimes switched around in this process, and from their standpoint, lower priority schools actually funded.

Source Consultations with Ministry of Finance officials.

Procurement

The Development Policy and Planning Law allows SNGs to procure works, goods, and services if in compliance with the specified thresholds (Table 12), even if funded from the central budget.

Table 12: Procurement Thresholds

Form of Procurement	Threshold (MNT million)	
	Works	Goods and Services
Public tender	>80	>50
Price comparison or shopping	<80 and >10	<50 and >10
Direct	<10	<10

MNT = Mongolian togrog.
Source: Public Procurement Law 2005.

However, these provisions are often not complied with. *Soums* are prevented from assuming these functions by their *aimag* authorities and *aimags* by sector ministries or MOF. This centralizing tendency may often be for reasons linked to local capacity, but it does suggest that opportunities may sometimes be missed for sourcing to local suppliers and contractors and more effective local supervision of contract implementation.

Similarly, the Public Procurement Law allows scope for community contracting or force account implementation, although these are rarely used, even under the LDF. This may be due to insufficient practical guidance. Opportunities to generate seasonal employment in local communities seem to be underexploited.

When construction of infrastructure is underway, it is not entirely clear what the respective roles of the sector ministry, the *aimag* line departments, the SNG authorities, or local user groups are, in monitoring contractor performance, certifying payments to contractors, and approving and commissioning the completed asset. This again can be attributed to the lack of clarity and inconsistencies between the provisions of the LATUG and the Law on Construction.

Asset Management

Under LATUG 2006, SNGs *hurals*, especially at the *soum* level, are mandated as legal owners of local socioeconomic facilities once completed and which should be included in the *soum* asset register. However, property transfer arrangements for existing schools, kindergartens, and water systems have often not been effected, especially transfers to *soums* by *aimag* authorities due to unclear procedures. Thus, *soum* SNG authorities are often unable to list them in their registers, nor can they exercise their infrastructure maintenance functions.[17]

The operation and maintenance of investment assets are compromised by the lack of integration of capital and recurrent budget decision-making, as outlined in Boxes 17, 18, and 19. For example, LDF investments such as streetlights or showers for *bagh* centers are often approved, but there is no corresponding recurrent budget commitment or revenue-raising device. Again, recourse may be made to enforced supplier credit from the power utility or to flexible resources such as the governor's reserve fund. Asset quality and services suffer as a result (Box 19).

Box 19: Issues Arising from Budget Execution and Asset Management

Subnational government spending has, to some extent, been a victim of the general government revenue shortfall issues seen in recent years. This has caused delays and compromised the quality of budget execution and service delivery.

Procurement of the investment budget has been centralized, thereby limiting the scope for local oversight and local multiplier effects. Opportunities for seasonal employment on works through community implementation or contracting under the Local Development Fund seem to have been lost.

The split between investment and current budget preparation and lack of guidance has meant that often assets created are not properly maintained, hence do not generate the expected services. Overall, there has been a lack of central guidance given to personnel in subnational governments on how to manage procurement and asset management and maintenance within the public financial management legal and regulatory framework.

Source: Consultations with local government officials.

---

[17] See detailed findings in this regard from the Energy Efficiency Project in B. Munkhsoyol and L. Otgontuya. 2014. *Research Report on Decision-Making on Investment in Public Assets: Roles and Responsibilities of Stakeholders.* Ulaanbaatar. GIZ/SDC.

BROADER SUBNATIONAL GOVERNMENT ROLES IN LOCAL DEVELOPMENT

This section explores the broader role for SNGs to address challenges in local settings through various levers of public action and the constraints they face. The three main areas relate to the challenges of urbanization, promotion of local economic development, and conserving the local environment in mining areas. These roles entail the use of SNG regulatory and convening powers.

The challenges around the core tasks of financing, planning, and delivery of basic socioeconomic services have been outlined in Section 2. However, there are several other local development challenges in Mongolia specific to local settings. The main constraints can be summarized under these headings:

(i)   managing urban development,

(ii) promoting local economic development, and

(iii) regulating extractive industries and conserving the environment.

Not all these challenges are amenable to public action through the state. Among those that are, the SNGs as the local arm of the state have a major role to play. Below we outline the potential SNGs have through levers for local public action and the constraints they face.

A. Managing Urban Development

1. Challenges and Opportunities

Mongolia has experienced rapid urbanization with a 6.3% annual increase in the population of Ulaanbaatar and, to a lesser extent, in secondary urban centers (Figure 8). These trends will continue in the decades ahead.

There is a range of factors driving these dynamics. The most common are the limited livelihood opportunities in rural areas, which is compounded by the episodic but often catastrophic *dzuds*; the growing aspirations among the young, associated with relatively high rates of educational attainment; and the appeal of broadcasted images of urban life.

A further major drawback is the legal provision that all citizens moving to urban areas are entitled to a free plot of land up to 700 square meters. This is perhaps the most generous such provision anywhere in the world.[18]

---

18   This provision derives from the Law on Land Allocation for Mongolian Citizens for Ownership (2002). See World Bank. 2015. Land Administration and Management in Ulaanbaatar, Mongolia.

Figure 8: Urbanization Trends
(million)

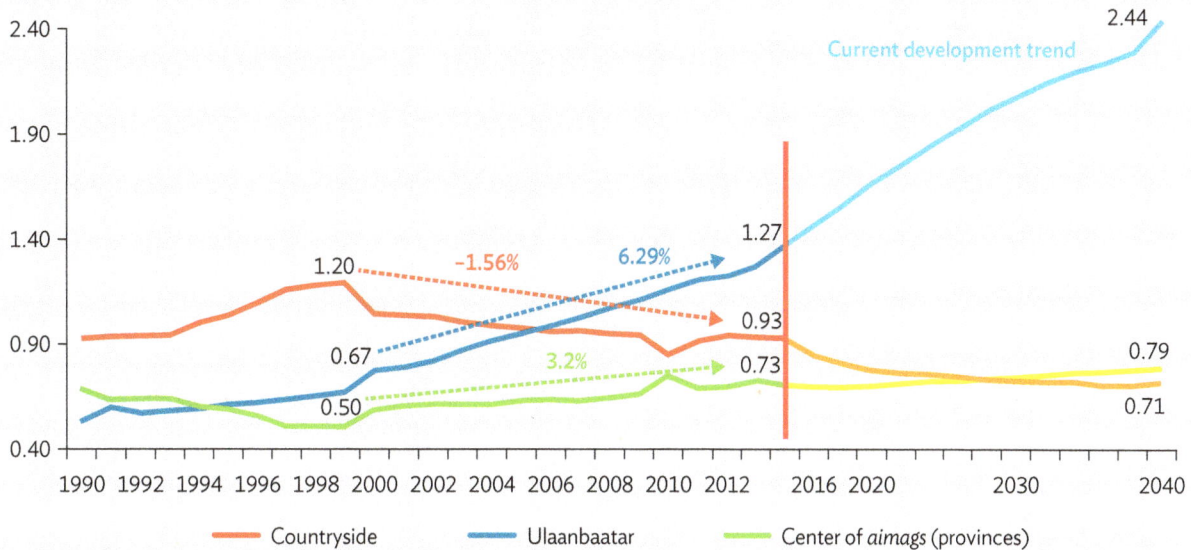

Source: Mongolia Habitat-III National Report (2016).

This has led a characteristic of urban growth in Ulaanbaatar and in secondary centers, which is rapid growth in low-density *ger* areas around the urban centers where each household lives on a family plot.

◼ Urban Land Use and Spatial Planning

Aside from public service delivery, a major role of urban SNGs is the management of public land and regulation of private land use and land markets, which directly shapes the spatial patterns and quality of housing, trade and industrial development, transport, and the overall urban environment.

A number of challenges are seen in Mongolia, especially in Ulaanbaatar, but to a growing extent in secondary centers.[19] For Ulaanbaatar, these challenges have been described in a recent ADB report:[20]

> The strategic urban infrastructure and planning are inadequate. The Municipality of Ulaanbaatar (MUB) needs to build its capacity to plan, regulate, and implement its urban development to overcome long-term economic, social, and environmental problems and to improve the people's quality of life. Parliamentary approval of the Ulaanbaatar Urban Development Master Plan 2030 in February 2013 and adoption of new laws to regulate the urban development of Ulaanbaatar provided a framework for the city's development. However, the existing technical capacity and institutional arrangements for urban planning in the MUB make it difficult to implement the master plan effectively and are inadequate for the urban development requirements of the rapidly growing city.

---

19   This subsection draws on World Bank (2015).

20   ADB. 2013. *Technical Assistance to Mongolia for the Ulaanbaatar Urban Planning Improvement.* Manila. p. 1.

Urban Planning Regulations

Current regulations are said to be rigid and discourage the mixed land use that international experience suggests as more appropriate, promoting instead excessive segregation between residential and commercial areas of the city and denying many of the potential socioeconomic benefits of agglomeration that normally accrue to both households and businesses in cities. To illustrate, under the Ulaanbaatar Master Plan, single-use residential zones are planned for 30% of the city (as against the 10%–15% suggested in UN Habitat 2013),[21] but no commercial activities are allowed. This adds to consumer transaction costs and time and discourages commercial business investments and employment. Box 20 describes urban planning and governance in various agencies.

Box 20: Urban Planning and Governance, a Multiplicity of Agencies

The Ministry of Construction and Urban Development is responsible for preparing the legal framework for urban planning, including laws on urban development, land management, construction, and for reviewing and approving the Ulaanbaatar urban plans before submission to Parliament.

- The Master Planning Agency of Capital City of MUB is responsible for (i) formulating policies on urban development, land administration, and infrastructure; (ii) preparing master plans and detailed development plans; (iii) developing the urban planning database; and (iv) monitoring development and construction activities. The agency has a division that manages the geographic information system and urban database.
- The Urban Planning, Architecture, and Design Institute is an agency under the Master Planning Agency of Capital City and is responsible for formulating the city's master plan, associated detailed plans, and building and infrastructure design according to the economic and social objectives of the city.
- Several other central agencies, such as the National Development Agency, are also involved in urban planning and implementation. Sector agencies are responsible for developing their sector master plans, such as the water and wastewater master plan, transport master plan, and energy master plan.
- Other sector ministries develop projects, plans, or regulations affecting Ulaanbaatar.

An example of institutional overlap between national city mayors and *aimag*-center *soum* administrations is Darkhan City co-terminus with Darkhan *soum* (population: 75,000).

Darkhan-Uul *aimag*

- Governor is also ex-officio mayor of Darkhan City
- Governor's Office has seven departments, including the Mayoral Support Department with units for power, infrastructure, urban services, and environment
- 21 deconcentrated *aimag* (province) sector departments and agencies
-
Darkhan (*aimag*–Center) *soum*

- Governor
- Governor's Office, including infrastructure and environment departments
- Deconcentrated *soum* (district) departments and agencies

Source: Consultations with central and local government officials.

---

21   https://unhabitat.org/planning-and-design-for-sustainable-urban-mobility-global-report-on-human-settlements-2013.

Uncertain and Opaque Land Administration

There have been frequent changes to the regulatory framework for land ownership and management, creating uncertainties and anomalies around the distinction between possession and ownership rights that have discouraged investment (Figure 9). These problems and uncertainties are exacerbated by the multiple agencies involved in land administration and by the considerable decision-making discretion given to SNG governors in changing land-right status or in extending the expiry date of permits.

As a consequence, many land users do not register their land, compromising both the state land registry and overall land management, as well as land-related revenue collection by SNGs. Investors are discouraged due to these land title uncertainties.

Figure 9: Procedures for Land Use, Possession, and Ownership Permits in Urban Area

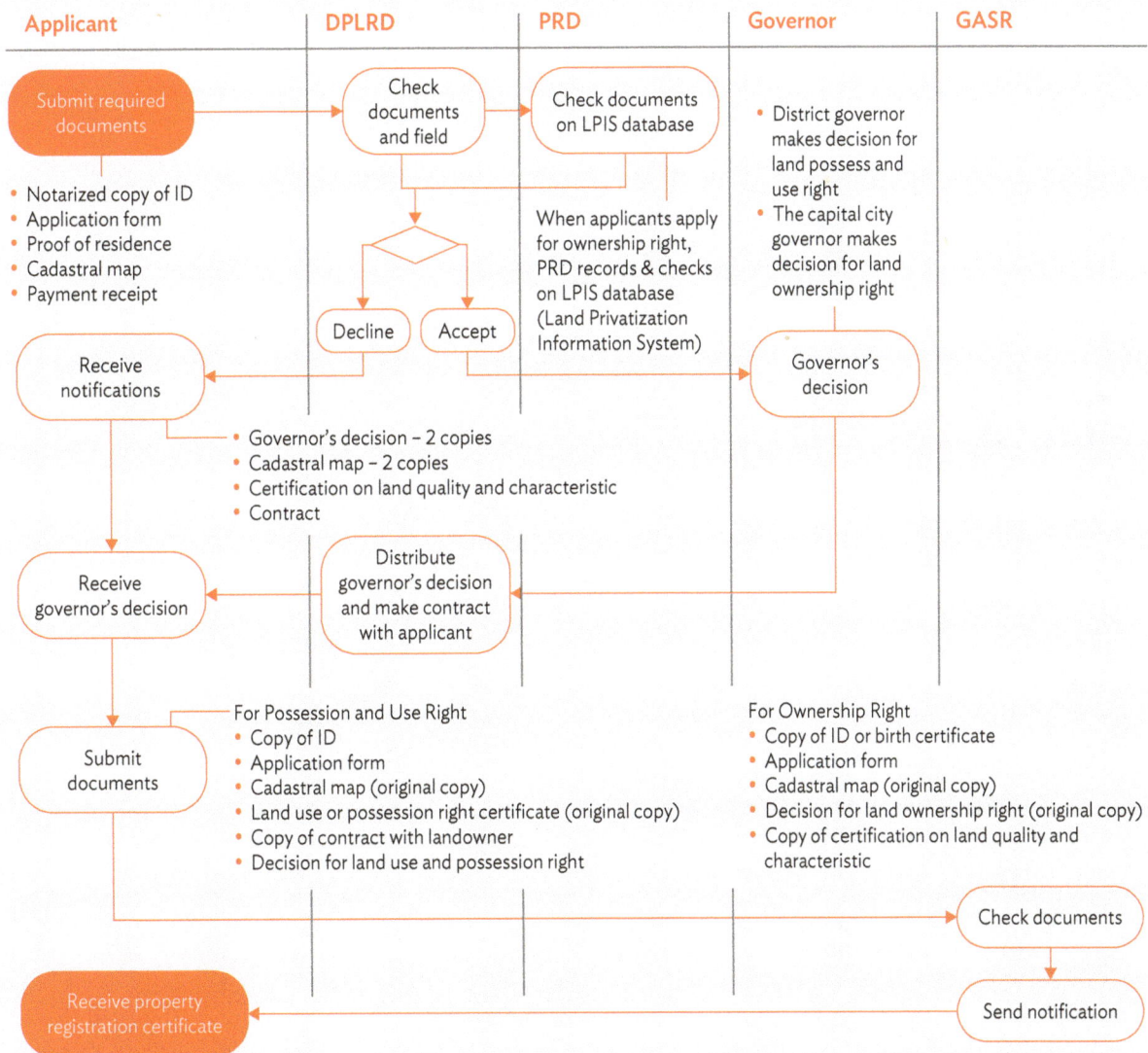

DPLRD = District Property and Land Relations Department, GASR = General Authority for State Registration, PRD = Property Relations Department.

Source: World Bank. 2015. *Land Administration and Management in Ulaanbaatar, Mongolia.* Washington, DC.

■ **Urban Service Delivery**

The rapid influx of migrants presents challenges in delivering services, especially in the relatively low-density *ger* peri-urban areas where migrants tend to settle. The relative disadvantages faced by the more sparsely populated Ulaanbaatar *ger* residents in accessing basic urban services emerge clearly from Table 13.

Table 13: Service Access by Location in Ulaanbaatar, 2014

| Service Type | Location/Dwelling Type[a] | | | |
	Peri-urban *ger* areas	Mid-tier *ger* areas	Central *ger*	Non-*ger* area
Tenure Status				
Possession or owner	62	63	57	56
Renter	4	6	15	11
No certificate	34	31	28	32
Total	**100**	**100**	**100**	**100**
Water Delivery				
Piped water	14	3	3	84
Kiosk connected to central pipeline	10	28	46	3
Tubewell and other	37	19	17	5
Kiosk with truck delivery	39	49	34	7
Total	**100**	**100**	**100**	**100**
Access to Toilet Facility				
Flush	13	2	4	84
Improved latrine	4	3	6	0
Unimproved or none	83	94	90	16
Total	**100**	**100**	**100**	**100**
Frequency of Garbage Collection				
Multiple collections per week	16	5	10	40
Multiple times per month	14	29	42	31
Once a month	32	44	38	8
Irregular or not collected	38	21	11	21
Total	**100**	**100**	**100**	**100**
Streetlight Functionality				
All or majority functional	24	26	32	60
A few work	6	17	15	14
None or non-functional	70	57	53	27
Total	**100**	**100**	**100**	**100**
Walking Distance to School				
15 minute or less	40	64	61	84
Greater than 15 minutes	60	36	39	16
Total	**100**	**100**	**100**	**100**

[a] *Ger* areas consist of households that live in a *ger* or detached house.

Sources: World Bank Survey. 2014; World Bank. 2017. *Toward Inclusive Service Delivery in Ulaanbaatar, Mongolia*. Washington, DC.

Survey data also showed that residents in outside *ger* areas report service access problems (e.g., for garbage collection, street lighting, water) with twice the frequency as residents of *ger* areas. This suggests that aside from the problems in supplying services to *ger* areas. An additional factor may be the relative weakness of citizen voice in those areas.

Urban Service Delivery: General Issues

In the Municipality of Ulaanbaatar (MUB) and other urban centers, services are mainly delivered through force accounts by public agencies.[22] Thus, Ulaanbaatar has 700 legal entities[23] and municipally-owned enterprises[24] delivering a wide range of services from water supply, garbage disposal, and street lighting to managing museums (see MUB organizational chart in Appendix 1, Figure A1.1). Aside from the rigidities and likely inefficiencies in force account arrangements, this multiplicity of agencies poses major coordination and service delivery monitoring problems for MUB and complicates the provision of feedback from citizens.

Solid Waste Management

Ulaanbaatar and other cities provide a basic waste collection service, with waste taken to landfill sites outside the urban area (Box 21). Collection frequency is usually low (often less than once per month per household), resulting in piles of uncollected waste with the attendant public health and environmental consequences. There is little or no recycling.

Box 21: **Waste Disposal in Darkhan City**

Responsibility: Darkhan city mayor (*aimag* [province] governor), not Darkhan *soum* (district) governor.

Service Mode: Force account by City Waste Management Department.

Enterprise Assets: Landfill site (10 kilometers outside the city), 1 bulldozer, 4 garbage trucks, 9 other old trucks, 165 staff.

Annual costs: MNT0.6 billion = 35% city urban services budget.

Investment Plan (unfunded): New landfill site, protected, guarded; recycling plant; more vehicles.

Source: Meetings with Darkhan City officials.

Heating

In all urban centers there are one or more publicly-owned thermal plants that circulate hot water to centrally located apartment buildings, offices, schools, and hospitals during the winter through an insulated pipe network. While this is feasible in densely populated areas with high-rise buildings, it is not economically feasible to extend these networks to surrounding low-density *ger* settlements.

---

[22] Force account: a payment method used for extra work when the contractor and a state agency cannot agree on a unit price or lump sum amount, or if either of those methods is impractical.

[23] It has been suggested that the large number is a reflection of the problems in closing agencies once they have been created. Source: World Bank. 2017. *Inclusive Service Delivery in Ulaanbaatar, Mongolia.* Washington, DC.

[24] Municipally-owned enterprises usually enter into some form of performance contract with MUB, but this is a pro forma arrangement that does not link payment to outputs but rather to inputs and activities.

Consequently, each *ger* household must provide its own heating, which is usually done by burning low-grade coal. This contributes to serious air pollution, and Ulaanbaatar is now considered one of the most polluted cities in the world (UNICEF 2018).[25] Air pollution is a general problem for all city residents but presents especially serious hazards for children and the elderly.

Drinking Water

In low-density *ger* areas, it is not feasible to provide piped water to all households. Instead, water is delivered through communal water kiosks, each serving around 1,000 people within a range of 100–500 meters. These kiosks are mainly supplied by pipes, but in some cases, by water tankers or from local wells. In most areas, this arrangement is adequate, but it imposes considerable access costs on households and limits the amount of water that can be consumed, especially for hygiene.[26]

Wastewater and Sanitation

There is no sewerage service to *ger* areas, and so *ger* households generally use latrines dug in their compounds. Household effluent is kept in pits below these latrines. Reports from some areas suggest this is beginning to leach into groundwater aquifers, posing a potentially serious public health problem as the population increases.

Streetlighting

Both MUB and its districts have legal mandates for provision and maintenance of streetlights. The city contracts Ulaanbaatar Netgel, a municipally-owned enterprise, for the central area, while districts in the outlying areas contract other city enterprises to provide lighting. *Khoroo* leaders are charged with identifying lighting and maintenance needs and submit requests to MUB or the districts for funding. Both MUB and the districts then develop their own plans and procure their own equipment. As a result, there are seven entities involved in street lighting across Ulaanbaatar and service quality varies greatly.[27]

Public Transport

Ensuring that residents in outlying *ger* areas of Ulaanbaatar have access to public transport remains a challenge. This is exacerbated by the relatively sparse settlement densities and by the number and the quality of the road links. MUB's public transit services are provided by private bus and taxi companies licensed by the Department of Transport. There are two major constraints to more accessible and efficient public transit: (i) an unbalanced road layout (a ratio of primary and secondary roads to local roads); and (ii) weak regulation of route planning, ticketing, and oversight of operators. For a city of its size, Ulaanbaatar and *ger* residents spend a disproportionate amount of time commuting or waiting for transport.

A new initiative supported by ADB aims to address these problems through measures including:[28] support to MUB Transport Department regulatory and oversight capacity, redesign of bus routes from simple radial

---

[25] https://www.unicef.org/eap/sites/unicef.org.eap/files/press-releases/eap-media-Mongolia_air_pollution_crisis_ENG.pdf. According to UN Habitat (2016), the *ger* areas contribute 60% of Ulaanbaatar's air pollution, as against 20% for motor vehicles. https://uploads.habitat3.org/hb3/Mongolia-HABITAT-III-Report-25.04.2016-english-final.pdf.

[26] Consultations with SNG officials.

[27] UN Habitat. 2016. *Toward Inclusive Service Delivery in Ulaanbaatar, Mongolia.*

[28] See World Resources Institute. Undated. Presentation on Using Smart Card and GPS for Transit Policymaking in Ulaanbaatar. Washington, DC.

routes emanating from a single hub to a system of multiple local hubs linked to a central terminus, and introduction of e-ticketing and use of GPS for greater route efficiency and better monitoring.

2. Issues on Urban Management

SNGs face several issues and constraints in undertaking their various urban management and service delivery roles (Box 22).

Box 22: Issues Arising from Urban Management by Subnational Government

Institutional Proliferation and Coordination

One general constraint for Ulaanbaatar, and perhaps even more for other cities, is the lack of coordination between central government agency plans for urban centers and the urban subnational government (SNG) authorities, who may not be party to the central investment or other decisions taking place in their areas of jurisdiction.

Unclear Legal Status of Urban Authorities

Under the Law on Administrative and Territorial Units and Their Governance and the Budget Law, there is uniformity of statutes and responsibilities assigned to all SNGs at each tier. SNGs in urban areas are thus deprived of those mandated responsibilities and regulatory and other powers needed to address the specific service delivery and governance issues faced in urban areas such as congested, high-density settlements that have high densities of economic activity and security and safety problems, and thus with a range of social and environmental externalities to be addressed.

Internal Overlaps and Coordination Issues within City Administrations

For the national cities, there is an odd overlap in the respective roles of the mayor (the *aimag* [provincial] governor), and the *aimag*-center *soum* authorities, with duplication of responsibilities and staffing. For example, in Darkhan City, the mayoral office has departments that replicate departments in the *soum* (district) Governor's Office. Darkhan City and Darkhan *Aimag* are co-terminus.

Other duplication problems are seen within the Ulaanbaatar administration where, for example, the mayor has established eight district-level public outreach offices which overlap with the role of the respective district governors.

Regulatory Framework

The regulations on land-use zoning and land-use permits are rigid, cumbersome, and not conducive to the best mix of land use and development.

Urban Service Supply Rigidities

The various urban services under SNG authority are mainly delivered by a public entity or municipally-owned enterprise. This may not always be the most efficient way to manage these services, and some form of outsourcing could be more efficient, allow more flexibility in resource use, and greater scope to mobilize private funding for the necessary investments. However, there will be political obstacles to move in this direction. On the one hand, as seen in Darkhan, there are significant numbers of people on the public payroll. On the other hand, any private management, whether for solid waste management or other urban service, would almost certainly entail a rise in user fees by local *hurals*, which would be difficult to approve.

Urban Service Pricing Policies

Most services are provided in return for a user fee, but at rates that are usually well below economic cost, i.e., they fail to cover either capital costs or recurrent staff and other costs entailed in delivering services. Instead, these are covered under the costs of the general SNG administrations concerned. The consequence is that user-fee revenues are insufficient to improve services to current urban populations and certainly not adequate to make the necessary investments to expand them to meet the needs of a growing urban population. That said, it is probably unrealistic to expect that local *hurals* (elected assemblies) will agree to raise user fees given their unpopularity and the underlying expectation that "funds can be found" from the governor's reserve funds or the central government when they are really needed, as is the case in other areas of local revenue shortfall.

Source: Consultations with local government officials.

B. Governments Promoting Local Economic Development

1. Challenges and Opportunities

There are different sets of local economic challenges in urban and rural areas. In Ulaanbaatar and other urban centers, SNGs need to promote employment for the growing population, especially for the growing number of young school-leavers, while taking care to regulate business development and land use and the related social and environmental externalities.

The mirror image of rapid urbanization is population loss in rural areas, especially among the younger and better educated. Much of this is the product of a low productivity livestock-based economy and economic trends that the state or the SNGs can do little to counter. However, there is some modest scope for local public action to mitigate the effects and slow the exodus, both to support existing pastoral-based economic activity and to support some degree of local diversification.

To that end, SNG authorities prepare economic development policies and plans. Govisumber *aimag*, for example, has prioritized the development of livestock processing, brown coal mining and processing, and electric power production and transmission. Darkhan-Uul *aimag* has prioritized development of business activity around its university and research institutes in Darkhan City, investment in tanneries for hide processing, and promoting intensive agriculture in neighboring *soums*. It has also prioritized investment in waste disposal and recycling technology (Box 23).

Box 23: Sustainable Development Councils

Under the Integrated Mineral Resource Initiative (IMRI), GIZ is supporting pilot multi-stakeholder business development platforms called sustainable development councils in three *aimags* (provinces of Ovs, Selenge, and Bayankhongor). These bodies are established by a decision of the *aimag hural* (provincial elected assembly), comprising 15 members representing the local business community and chaired by the *aimag hural* chair. Its purpose is to act as an advisory body to the *hural* on matters of local economic and business development policy. Their running costs are funded by the *hurals*, with external training in local economic development from GIZ.

If successful, the aim is to work with the Cabinet Secretariat to replicate sustainable development councils in all *aimags* as mandatory economic development advisory bodies to the *aimag hurals*.

Under the Integrated Mineral Resource Initiative (IMRI), GIZ is supporting the piloting of multi-stakeholder business development platforms called sustainable development councils in three *aimags* (Ovs, Selenge, and Bayankhongor). These bodies are established by decision of the *aimag hural*, comprising 15 members representing the local business community and chaired by the *aimag hural* chair, whose purpose is to act as advisory bodies to the hural itself on matters of local economic and business development policy. Their running costs are funded by the *hurals*, with external training in local economic development from GIZ.

If proven successful, the aim is to work with Cabinet Secretariat to replicate these sustainable development councils in all *aimags*, as mandatory economic development advisory bodies to the *aimag hurals*.

GIZ = Deutsche Gesellschaft für Internationale Zusammenarbeit.
Source: Asian Development Bank.

Whatever the quality of the local economic plan or policy, implementation depends on the role SNGs can actually play and on the levers of public action at their disposal. In principle, SNGs have several potential levers to promote economic development in urban and rural areas.

◾ Spending on Local Public Investments and Services

Spending on local public investments and services is based on devolved or delegated functional mandates and financed by the respective SNG budgets. These entail public spending on local services and infrastructure (public or merit goods) in which the private sector will underinvest. This may be spending on:

(i)   education, health, water, and other social services and infrastructure, to improve human well-being and developing human capital delivery and access;

(ii) economic services and investments to promote local economic development (e.g., roads, industrial areas, power generation or distribution, pasture improvement and fencing, farm extension, and veterinary services).

Such spending may also be directed preferentially to local suppliers and contractors or to local communities in the case of small public works. In providing such services, SNGs may also leverage their ownership of public assets. As part of the socialist heritage, SNGs are often owners of public assets and property currently unused or underused. These assets can be put to good use (e.g., state land could be allocated for business development, waste disposal, or public parks), and former military buildings could be converted into office space, schools, or cultural centers.

◾ Regulatory Powers

Subnational governments enjoy some powers:

(i)   Issue business permits: trade-specific permits to open and operate a business, issued by the sector department concerned (only in Ulaanbaatar and at *aimag* level).

(ii)   Issue land-use permits and rules, land use, ownership or possession titles for citizens and businesses, whether in rural or urban areas; issued by SNG governors at all levels who enjoy considerable discretion in these approvals.

(iii) Facilitate legally mandated registration and access to registry documents for both citizens and businesses by opening local one-stop-service shops, business centers, or other channels.

(iv)   Ensure zoning of economic and land-use activity to ease congestion, mitigate pollution, and promote economies of agglomeration.

(v)   Ensure due controls over natural resource extraction.

(vi)   Support local collective arrangements (e.g., pasture management by herders).

These powers can be used to provide incentives through decisions regarding extending land-use permits and invoking delegated powers to subsidize nighttime power tariffs for citizens or businesses.

■ Convening Powers

SNGs also enjoy powers to bring stakeholders together to plan and make decisions about local development issues for which ordinarily they may not meet or communicate; for example:

(i)   groups of herders and farmers meet to agree on common land or pasture management issues;

(ii) groups of business people meet to agree on joint investment in common facilities, relocation, or to gather collective views on future economic development policy; and

(iii) mining companies and residents meet to resolve conflicts.

2. Issues in Local Economic Development

SNGs face several constraints and limitations on their potential role in promoting local economic development through the levers outlined in Section 2 and summarized in Box 24.

Box 24: Role of Subnational Governments in Local Economic Development: Issues and Constraints

Economic Investment and Services

The investment budget resources of subnational governments (SNGs) are limited and non-Local Development Fund (LDF) investment is under tight central control. Even where SNGs are able to undertake investments, they face constraints:

- Investments in urban areas are often selected by external planning consultants on the basis of an idealized master plan template rather than through a more context-driven and consultative process.
- There are currently no useful guidelines to assist SNGs in the technically difficult task of identifying and appraising investment projects on the basis of socioeconomic merit and development impact. This divide between capital and recurrent budgeting processes often compromises the sustainability of investments.
- There is a lack of clarity around the appropriate strategic role of public investment funding and a temptation for SNGs to invest in projects best left to the private sector.
- Opportunities to maximize local multiplier effects are limited insofar as procurement for larger projects is often managed at the central level, and local contractors may miss out.
- A number of urban public services, for example, waste disposal, could be managed in ways that would allow for more effective service delivery and possibly offer more opportunities for private sector development.

Similarly, basic service delivery to support economic sectors, such as veterinary services for livestock herders, is constrained by the recurrent budget norms, which can greatly limit the flexibility of sector service staff to respond to needs or to travel.

Regulation and Incentives

There are few discretionary incentives that SNGs can offer to encourage business development. The one area where SNGs appear to have discretionary authority is over the issuance and extension of land-use permits. Here too, there are limitations:

- Urban land-use regulations are rigid and do not encourage multi-use patterns that would be incentives for business development.
- Land-use permits are governed by a range of institutions, and the issuance and approval procedures are slow.
- Although SNG governors appear to enjoy considerable discretion, it is not clear that they receive sufficient policy guidance on how to use this discretion effectively and equitably.

One area where SNGs have made considerable effort is in the opening of one-stop public service centers to simplify the issuance of business permits and payment of taxes. Several countries have sent missions to observe these initiatives.

Source: Consultations with local government officials.

One issue emerging from a recent survey is the apparent variance in the way that SNGs actually use their local regulatory powers to promote local economic development.[29] This is reflected in the aggregate government efficiency performance ratings from the SLP3-MOF annual performance assessment for all 330 *soums*. It can be seen in two specific local business climate-related measures as shown in Box 25.

This variance in the business climate suggests some scope for improvement among the poorer performing *aimags* through the promotion of local SNG awareness and capacities to use their regulatory powers more effectively to promote local business activity.

Box 25: **Variance in Local Regulatory Climate for Business**

Provincial administrative regulations   **2017**

Administrative regulations by local government support creation of favorable business environment.

Survey

Ranking		0–10 scores
1	Orkhon	5.00
2	Dornogobi	4.89
3	Tuv	4.47
4	Bayankhongor	4.39
5	Selenge	4.33
6	Uvs	4.23
7	Darkhan-Uul	4.22
8	Khentii	4.19
9	Sukhbaatar	4.18
10	Khuvsgul	4.14
11	Uvurkhangai	4.11
12	Bulgan	4.09
13	Bayan-Ulgii	4.02
14	Dornod	3.98
15	Govisumber	3.97
16	Gobi-Altai	3.88
17	Dundgovi	3.68
18	Zavkhan	3.51
19	Arkhangai	3.50
19	Umnugovi	3.50
21	Khovd	3.18

Licenses   **2017**

Licensing requirements for businesses are well-understood and easily accessible.

Survey

Ranking		0–10 scores
1	Dornogobi	4.78
2	Uvurkhangai	4.50
3	Tuv	4.43
4	Khovd	4.25
5	Darkhan-Uul	4.15
6	Bayan-Ulgii	4.12
7	Selenge	4.02
7	Orkhon	4.02
9	Uvs	4.00
10	Dornod	3.90
11	Bulgan	3.88
12	Sukhbaatar	3.84
13	Khentii	3.70
14	Govisumber	3.68
15	Bayankhongor	3.61
15	Khuvsgul	3.58
17	Gobi-Altai	3.39
18	Zavkhan	3.24
19	Umnugovi	3.22
20	Dundgovi	2.91
21	Arkhangai	3.24

Source: Economic Policy and Competitiveness Research Center. 2017. *Mongolia: Provincial Competitiveness Report 2017*. Ulaanbaatar.

[29]   See Economic Policy and Competitiveness Research Center. 2017. *Mongolia: Provincial Competitiveness Report 2017*. Ulaanbaatar.

C. Regulating Extractive Industries and Conserving the Environment

1. Context and Challenges

Since 2000, the mining sector has grown rapidly and now accounts for 20% of GDP, 86% of exports, and employs 60,000–70,000 people. As of 2016, there were approximately 2,000 exploration and 1,550 production licenses for large international companies, together with smaller nationally-owned mining operations issued for operations covering 13.5 million hectares. The majority are in 10 of the 21 *aimags*.

Since 2007, Mongolia has been a member of the global Extractive Industries Transparency Initiative (EITI), which aims to promote transparency and accountability in this sector, given its dominance in the economy. In compliance with EITI commitments, there are now regular public reports on mining company operations and their licensing, on revenues generated, and on revenue-sharing arrangements at the local level.

Major concerns have been raised regarding the local environmental and social costs of these extractive operations. SNGs have been accorded a significant role in the measures designed to address these concerns.

■ Legal Framework and Role of Subnational Government

Mining Legislation

A detailed body of laws has been developed to regulate the mining sector:

(i) The Minerals Law of Mongolia (2006) governs certain aspects of the mineral exploration and production licensing regime.

(ii) The Subsoil Law of Mongolia (1988) regulates the use and protection of subsoil, including in the construction of underground mining operations and facilities.

(iii) The Environmental Protection Law of Mongolia (1995) sets out the administrative framework and general obligations relating to environmental matters.

(iv) The Environmental Impact Assessment Law of Mongolia (2012) sets out the framework and obligations relating to the measurement and reporting of the impact of projects on the environment.

All licensing under this framework is administered primarily through the Ministry of Mining and Heavy Industry and the Mineral Resources and Petroleum Authority of Mongolia.

However, SNG authorities also have an important legally mandated role under the Minerals and the Environmental Laws in regulating this sector and managing related environmental issues. This is in addition to their responsibilities for spending on environmental protection and conservation services devolved to *aimag* and *soum* SNGs under the Budget Law.

■ The Regulatory and Oversight Challenge for Subnational Governments

Issuance of Land Permits

All foreign-owned mining companies must negotiate a land possession or use agreement with the SNG authority of the relevant *soum* and obtain a land use or possession certificate from that authority.

Issuance of Water Permits

All mining companies must obtain water-use permits under the Law on Water (2002). The daily water quantity is determined by the issuing authority:

(i)   fewer than 50 cubic meters: *soum* governor;

(ii) 50–100 cubic meters: *aimag* environment office; and

(iii) over 100 cubic meters: regional water basin authority.

Once issued, a permit is valid for 10 years and subject to compliance with the terms of a water-use contract. It may be extended for a 5-year period. In addition to the water permit, the license-holder must enter into a water-use contract either with the issuing authority or another water supply organization. The water-use contract will set out the terms, including rights of termination and fees, to which the holder's water use is subject.

Environmental Conservation

For the environmental management plan (EMP) and reporting, the license-holder must first adopt an EMP detailing measures to mitigate environmental contamination. For exploration licenses, the governor of the *soum* in which the license area is located must approve the EMP. For mining licenses, approval must be obtained from the Ministry of Environment and Tourism.

The license-holder must also provide annual reports on implementing the EMP to the Environment Monitoring Department of the relevant *soum* and *aimag* (for exploration licenses) or the Ministry of Environment and Tourism (for mining licenses).

Second, under Articles 38, 39, and 40 of the Minerals Law, the license-holder must deposit 50% of the budget set aside in its EMP in a reclamation fund administered by the governor of the relevant *soum* or *aimag* in the case of an exploration license, and with the Ministry of Environment and Tourism in the case of a mining license. This is to guarantee the performance of its obligations under the EMP.

If a mining license-holder breaches the obligation to deposit funds into the reclamation fund before starting the mining operation, the governor of the relevant *soum* may suspend the holder's operations. Upon closure of its mine and provided it has met its obligations under the EMP and its environmental impact assessment, a license-holder is entitled to be refunded any contributions made to the reclamation fund.

Local-level Agreements

The Minerals Law (Article 42.1) requires that a mining license-holder "works in cooperation with the local administrative bodies and establishes agreements on environmental protection, mine exploitation, and infrastructure development in relation to mine development and job creation." For this purpose, a model local-level agreement (LLA) was developed as a template in 2016.

2. Regulation and Environmental Conservation Issues

While the recognition of a role for local authorities in the governance of mining activities is positive, what appears to be lacking is clear guidance on how to implement legal provisions such as:[30]

(i)   Determine when issuance of land or water permits for mining is or is not appropriate in light of possible environmental or social consequences.

(ii)   Review and monitor company environmental management plans or learn how to use the reclamation fund they should be receiving to finance these plans based on the types of expenditures eligible and most effective, and learn how to plan, budget, implement, and report on such expenditures. Lacking such guidance, these funds often revert to general SNG revenues and are spent on other things.

(iii)   Negotiate an LLA or EMP, a process in which they are often at a considerable negotiating disadvantage. There is no clarity as to the respective roles of *soum* and *aimag* authorities, or of the role of the *hurals* at each level in the process. As a result, there is considerable variance in practice between *aimags*.

An extensive review by the Natural Resource Governance Institute indicates that the prescribed LLAs are often not established, and when they are formally agreed, they are often not put into practice by the companies or not reported on. A recent review in Khentii *Aimag* suggested that for the 273 licenses issued, there appeared to be only 10 LLAs. In Sukhbaatar *Aimag*, for 127 licenses, only one LLA was established. The larger foreign-owned companies seem to see more incentives to negotiate LLAs than national and state-owned companies. One major obstacle is that establishing an LLA is not a precondition for the issuance of a license by the Mineral Resources and Petroleum Authority of Mongolia, but only a nonbinding follow-up step. Furthermore, there are no sanctions for noncompliance in place despite pressure by CSOs for such measures to be introduced.

Generally, *aimag* and *soum* governors and staff report they are not always sure how to delineate their mandated roles from deconcentrated state environmental inspectors deployed to *aimag* and *soums*, given the inconsistencies in provisions across the range of other sector-specific legal instruments governing this set of activities.

---

[30]   This section is sourced from B. Dalaibuyan. 2017. Local-level Agreements in Mongolia's Resource Sector: Lessons Learned and the Way Forward. *NRGI Briefing*; B. Dalaibuyan. Undated. Mining, 'Social License' and Local-Level Agreements in Mongolia. *Research Paper*. University of Queensland.

CONCLUSIONS AND FUTURE DIRECTIONS

A. Constraints Facing Subnational Governments in the Implementation of Their Responsibilities

Mongolian SNGs, like local authorities elsewhere, enjoy certain comparative institutional advantages and suffer comparative disadvantages in delivering public services and promoting local development in their areas of jurisdiction.

First, in contrast to local NGOs and CSOs, they have a broad development mandate and enjoy generally broad and uncontested legitimacy, legal backing, and permanence, as well as access to state resources. Second, compared to central government departments and agencies, (i) SNGs are potentially faced with much greater pressures for local accountability and results; (ii) they can potentially receive detailed regular information regarding locally variable problems, needs, priorities, and complaints; and (iii) they potentially may enjoy much greater ability to respond to these local context-variable needs and pressures in a flexible manner.

However, SNGs face constraints in achieving their potential. It is common to attribute these constraints to local capacity weaknesses, but this is a generic diagnosis and can be misleading. It suggests that the solution lies in more training rather than a need for more systemic changes and reforms. By international standards, SNGs in Mongolia employ substantial and competent human resources. While they do face staff capacity challenges, the primary constraints are in specific areas:

(i)   The policy, legal, and regulatory framework within which they must operate is sometimes internally inconsistent, sometimes offers perverse incentives, sometimes allows undue discretion, and is often not translated into clear operational guidance for SNGs.

(ii) The local institutional setup often duplicates functions and blurs accountabilities. This gives little scope for locally elected *hurals*, thus promoting a vicious cycle that compromises their potentially critical political and developmental role. This also prevents either the *hurals* or the SNG governors from exercising effective coordination or supervision over local deconcentrated staff.

(iii) The financing and budgeting arrangements impose a straitjacket precluding the kind of local discretion that is the rationale for decentralization. This undercuts the scope for input, supervision, and coordination over local sector departments by local authorities and, in some cases, allows for undue discretion and untransparent behavior (e.g., in *aimag* budgetary allocations to *soums*).

To address these constraints and allow SNGs to fulfill their potential, the following are necessary:

(i) **Improve delivery of basic local services.** Service delivery spending becomes ineffective in meeting location-specific needs and priorities when many responsibilities remain under the central government, when even those formally decentralized responsibilities are subject to centralized and rigid budget decision-making processes, and when there is little guidance on translating policy into spending practice. Service delivery is less equitable across SNG areas than it could be because of the great variance in resources per capita allocated between *soums* and *aimags*. Much could be done to improve efficiency in translating resources into service outputs, guidance, and incentives surrounding the budget process, and the problems in treasury and procurement. Basic local spending is less accountable than it could be when there are overlaps in local institutional oversight roles.

(ii) **Promote broader local development through regulatory and convening powers.** Local development is often limited due to the relatively weak powers assigned to SNGs. Regulatory and convening powers are compromised by inconsistent laws and regulations underlying these powers (e.g., as in the land-use framework). The frequent lack of clear guidance on their application further compromises regulation (e.g., as in the mining environmental management plans or LLA). Finally, the process results in less accountability because of unclear and overlapping local institutional oversight roles.

B. Some Directions for Subnational Government Development

1. Strengthening the Policy, Legal, and Regulatory Framework

The 2016 Government Resolution and the recently formed State *hural* working group provide an important opportunity to develop a clearer and more consistent national framework for subnational governance and service delivery. This could include:

(i) Establishment of an interministerial working group, chaired by the Cabinet Secretariat, to develop an action plan to implement the directions set out in the government resolution and to map the implications for the sector ministries concerned. As part of this exercise, the following specific policy themes should be explored and options examined.

   a. Legal provision should be made to recognize the specific challenges faced by urban SNGs in future revisions of the LATUG and the Budget Law to create asymmetries in regulatory and revenue-raising powers and spending responsibilities.

   b. Opportunities and challenges for the role, operation, and performance of SNGs should be embodied in recent pieces of legislation such as the Development Policy and Planning Law and the recently revised Civil Service Law.

   c. SNG expenditure responsibilities should be incorporated in the functional assignment policy approved by the Cabinet Secretariat and reflected in the revised Budget Law. There is a need to specify what functions are to be transferred and when, the nature of the desired form of decentralization (devolution or delegation), and the budget expenditure implications for SNGs.

It will be important to include sector capital spending in this exercise, not just recurrent spending.[31]

d. SNG revenues and transfers should cover the adequacy and equity of current arrangements in view of increased future SNG spending responsibilities, the scope for increasing the revenue powers of SNGs (sources and rate decision powers), and the scope for revising transfer mechanisms to allow greater transparency, equity, and SNG discretion, as might be achieved, for example by introducing simple formula-based conditional grants to finance the decentralized subsector responsibilities already agreed.

e. In SNG budgeting, the Medium-Term Fiscal Framework budget ceilings for base expenditures communicated to *aimags* in the Budget Circular should be respected in the budget proposals submitted to the central government. *Aimags*, in turn, should communicate budget ceilings to their *soums* to better discipline priority setting and to encourage budget cutback choices to be made locally rather than centrally. It is also important to provide similar advance budget ceilings to *aimags* and *soums* for delegated social expenditures.

f. The LDF appears to be in need of a review to clarify several policy issues such as (1) the nature of the eligible spending menus at *aimag* and *soum* levels and how they relate to future SNG sector capital spending, (2) the rationale for sharing mining royalty revenues by origin into LDF accounts in view of the inequities arising, and (3) and the rationale for the General Local Development Fund (GLDF) formula, which currently penalizes more highly populated SNGs and includes other inconsistencies and anomalies.

g. Regarding central monitoring of SNGs, the assumption when moving to greater decentralization is that the central government can better track and analyze SNG revenues and spending. This will require (1) more comprehensive and analytically useful reporting by *aimags* to MOF, including similar reporting on the *soums* (currently missing altogether); and (2) a focal unit for SNG finance within MOF to which all reports on transfers to SNGs, and SNG's own-revenues and sectoral expenditures are submitted. At the same time, consideration should be given to the appropriate forms of external audit and supervision by the Mongolian National Audit Office and State Inspection Agency to ensure that resources are used in a manner that provides for more regular and consistent audits than currently take place.

h. It is also important to review the scope for developing performance monitoring and incentive mechanisms for SNGs tied to fiscal transfers, building on those already practiced such as the performance-based grant and annual performance assessment, i.e., the annual performance appraisal mechanism being tested alongside the LDF under the Sustainable Livelihoods Project Phase 3 but for which a more sustainable mechanism urgently needs developing.

---

[31] Guidance in regard to functional assignment methodology can be found in R. Rohdewold. 2017. Localizing Global Agendas in Multilevel Governance Systems. *Governance Brief.* Issue No. 30. Manila: ADB.

i. Regarding the regulatory powers of SNGs, while discussion of SNG functions is equated with narrower spending responsibilities, the broader set of regulatory powers enjoyed by SNGs deserves a review. These are critical to several pressing issues related to urban governance, local economic development, and proper regulation of extractive industries. This review would focus on the adequacy of current powers and on possible regulatory unclarities or inconsistencies arising in exercising these powers.

(ii) Any future policy consultation and development on SNGs must include other voices to represent the views of SNG governors and *hurals* (possibly through the Mongolian Association of Local Authorities) and those of CSOs and NGOs working with SNGs. It would be useful if a forum were held on a periodic basis where stakeholders could interact with central government authorities and State *hural* members on policy around subnational governance.

2. Building Subnational Government Capacities

SNGs in Mongolia appear to need more proactive and sustainable support, even for exercising their existing responsibilities—all the more so if these responsibilities are to be increased. The support needed is of different types:

(i) **A mechanism to extend routine induction training and provide regular follow-up and refresher training to subnational government personnel (both *hural* members and officials).** This would cover their specific duties, policy, and legislation related to these duties and guidance on day-to-day handling of these duties using the guidelines below. This would require building the foundation with the National Academy of Governance under the UNDP–SDC CRH project, creating training-of-trainers teams and helpdesks at the *aimag* level (building on the SLP3 *aimag* team model), and ensuring there are earmarked government budgetary resources for these activities. The budget could be part supply-driven training on the central budget and part demand-driven arrangements that are flexible, with budgets under SNG control.

(ii) **Training materials such as practical guidelines and reference materials.** Much training to date is generic. To implement or comply with national policies, laws, and regulations, whether related to local planning, budgeting, service delivery, regulating the environment or local economic development, practical guidelines, and related case materials are needed to assist SNG personnel (whether officials or *hural* members). Some material of this sort has been developed in some areas under specific projects, however, this too is often generic. Institutional capacity to create, revise, and update such materials should be created, possibly within the NAOG or a similar training agency.

3. Promoting Local Accountability and Transparency

Historically, much of the donor, NGO, and CSO support to local governance has focused on promoting fora such as town hall meetings and monitoring transparency. These efforts could be further strengthened through the following means:

(i) Reform the financing mechanisms and budget norms to allow greater local discretion, the lack of which is perhaps the major impediment to any substantial degree of citizen and NGO engagement with SNGs.

(ii) Extend simple incentives associated with fiscal transfer arrangements to reward SNGs that make greater efforts and build on the SLP3 performance-based grant and annual performance assessment mechanisms.

(iii) Provide operational guidance to SNGs on how to implement the numerous existing legal provisions to mandate disclosure and engagement by SNGs (e.g., for participatory planning, procurement, monitoring of service delivery). Such guidance would need to feed into the institutionalized training programs suggested above.

(iv) Support and train CSOs and the media to encourage informed, investigative, and analytic coverage of SNG affairs.

APPENDIX 1
FINANCING, BUDGET, AND OTHER DATA

Figure A1.1: Ulaanbaatar Administration and Municipal Entities Under Its Authority

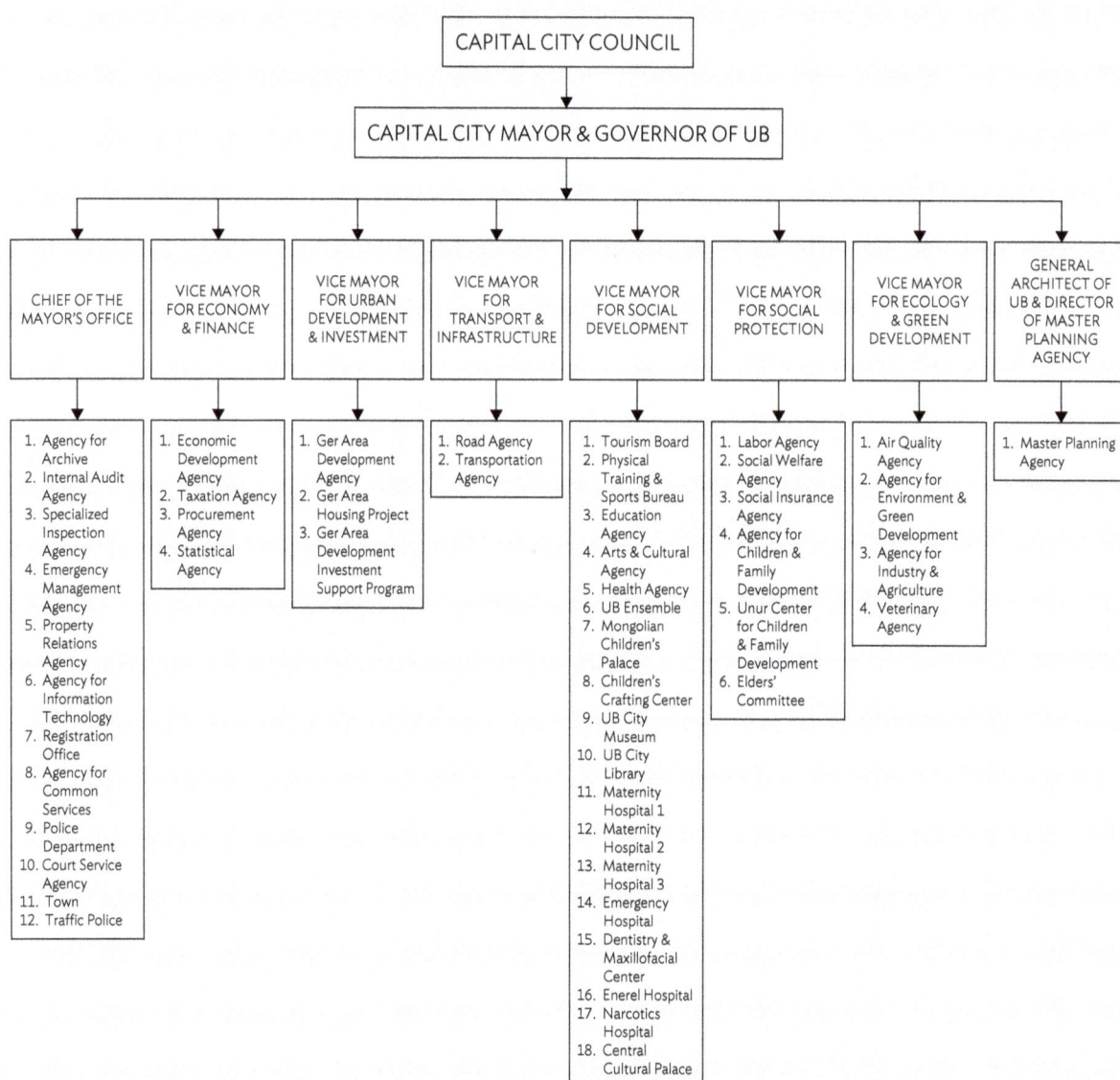

UB = Ulaanbaatar.
Source: World Bank. 2017. *Toward Inclusive Urban Service Delivery in Ulaanbaatar, Mongolia*. Washington, DC.

Figure A1.2: Local Development Fund Outcomes of Funding

Outcomes for Funding Local Development Fund Transfer Mechanism

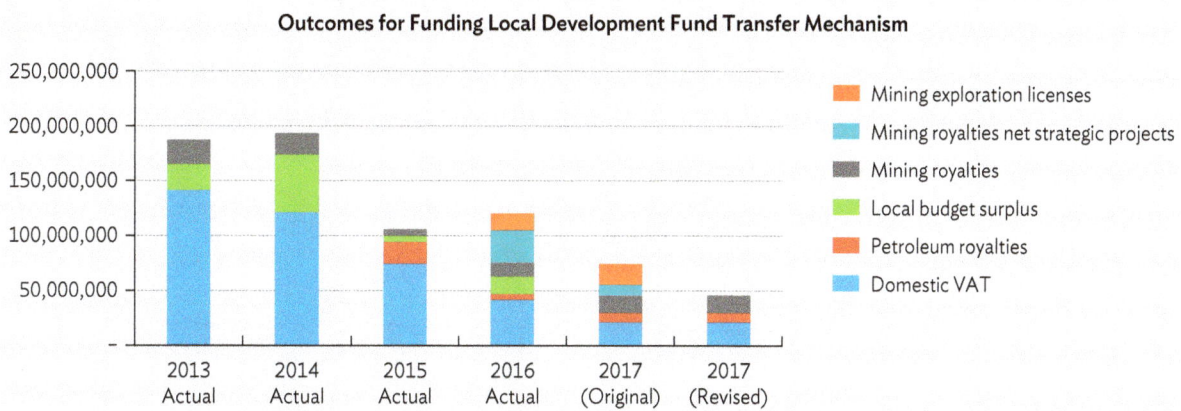

Outcomes for Local Development Fund: Funding at *Aimag* and *Soum* Levels

LDF Sub-pools for *Aimags* and *Soums*

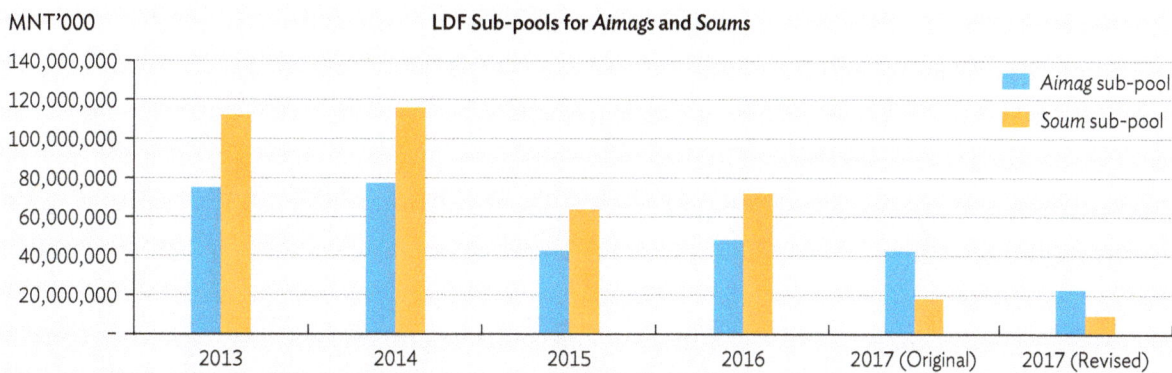

Variance of *Soum* Local Development Fund: Per Capita Funding in 2016

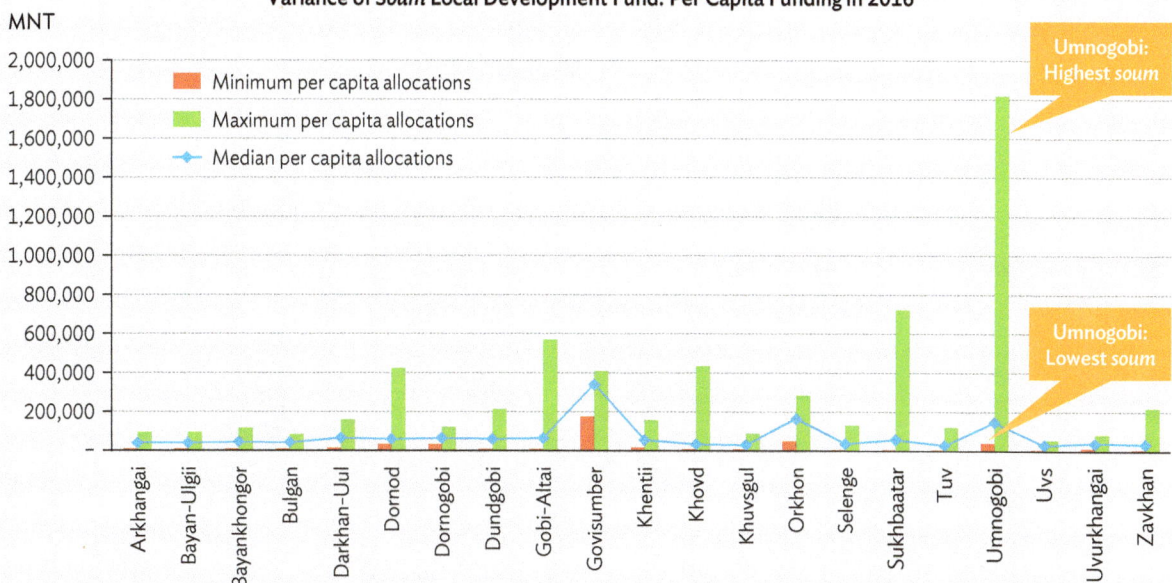

LDF = Local Development Fund.
Source: Data from Ministry of Finance officials.

Figure A1.3: *Soum* **Performance, 2016–2019**

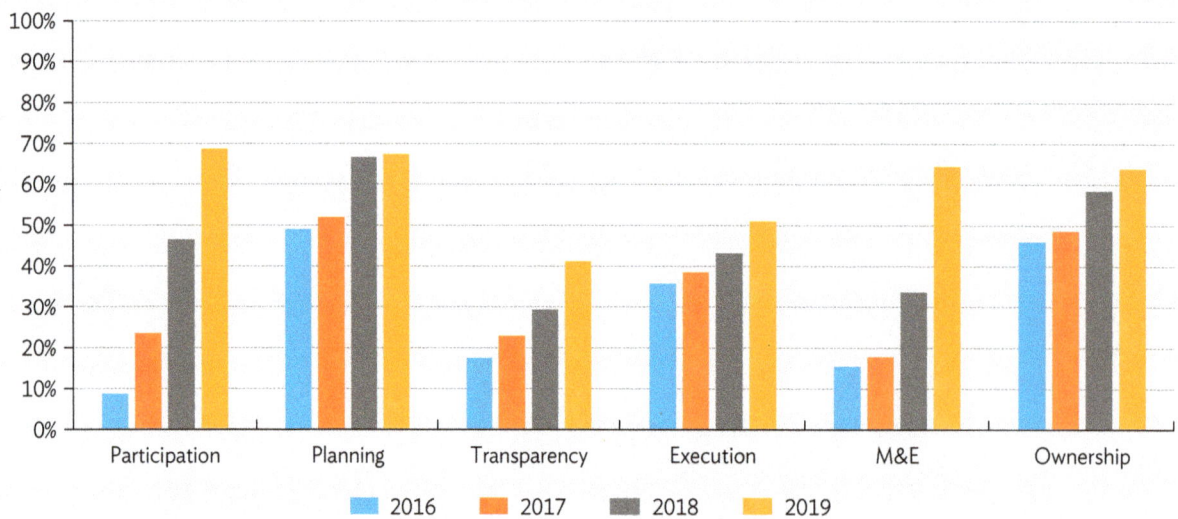

M&E = monitoring and evaluation.
Source: Data from Ministry of Finance. *PIU for Sustainable Livelihood Project Phase 3*. Ulaanbaatar.

Figure A1.4: Average Performance Rate in the Annual Performance Assessment by Section, 2016–2017

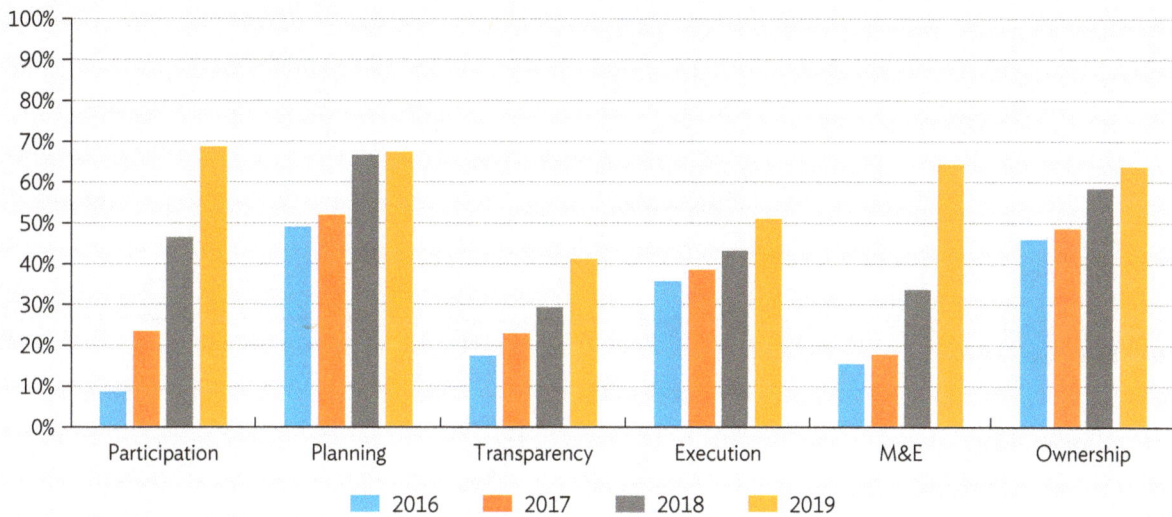

M&E = monitoring and evaluation.

Source: Data from Ministry of Finance. *PIU for Sustainable Livelihood Project Phase 3*. Ulaanbaatar.

Figure A1.5: Breakdown of Ulaanbaatar and District Current Expenditures, FY2013

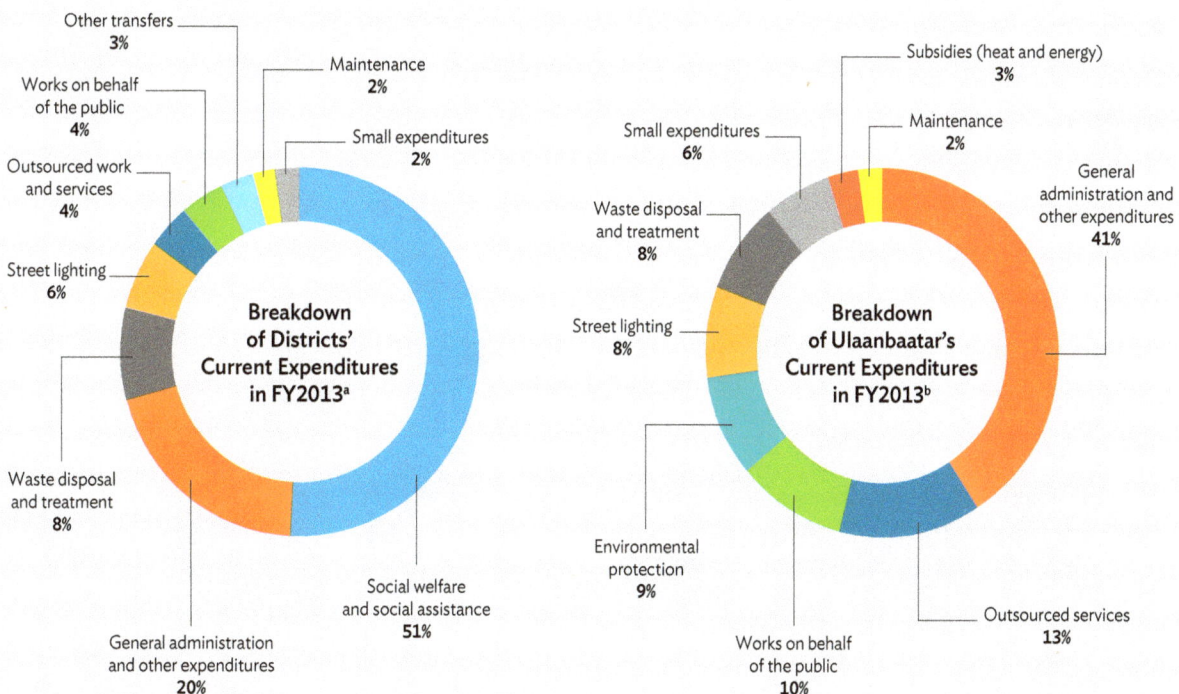

FY = fiscal year.

a World Bank staff calculations based on districts' budget for FY2013.

b World Bank staff calculations based on Ulaanbaatar City's executed budget for FY2013.

Figure A1.6: **Procedures, Times, and Costs in the Ulaanbaatar Land Privatization Process**

= 10,000 togrog   = 1,000 togrog   = 1 day   30 = 30 days

Steps	Cost (togrog)	Time Required	Organization in Charge
Cadastral map surveying	50,000	1 1 1	Surveying Company
Take municipality letter	100	1	Municipality
Print out cadastral map	2,500	1	UB City Land Office, Bank
Take the application form from District PRD	300	1	District Land Office, Bank
Certify documents	10,000	1	Notary
PRD at city level and DPLRD at district level check application	No Cost	1	UB City PRD Office
UB City governor decision	No Cost	30 30 30	UB City Governor
Take the decision certificate	No Cost	1	District PRD Office
Register at GASR	No Cost	14	GASR
TOTAL	62,900	30 30 30 23	

DPLRD = District Property and Land Relations Department, GASR = General Authority for State Registration, PRD = Property Relations Department, UB = Ulaanbaatar.

Note: Authors' compilation based on interviews.

Source: World Bank. 2015. *Land Administration and Management in Ulaanbaatar, Mongolia.* Washington, DC.

Table A1.1: The Local Development Fund: Instability and Inequity

1. Changing Funding Sources			
Revenue Source for LDF	When Introduced and Effective	Budget Law Article	Allocation Basis: Formula or by Origin
GLDF – Window I: Formula			
Value-added tax (domestic)	Included 2011, effective 2013	59.1.1 59.3	GLDF Formula (4 Criteria) Budget Law 59.3
Foreign aid and NGOs	Included 2011, effective 2013	59.1.3 56.2, 59.3	GLDF Formula (4 Criteria) Budget Law 59.3
Budget surplus (Article 56.2)	Annulled September 2016, effective FY2017	59.1.4 59.3	GLDF Formula (4 Criteria) Budget Law 59.33
Petroleum royalties	Included July 2014, effective FY2015	59.1.5 59.3	GLDF Formula (4 Criteria) Budget Law 59.3.3
GLDF – Window II: Formula + Origin			
Mineral royalties	Included 2011, effective 2013	59.1.2 59.4	Equal per capita rule but with 10% premium for area of origin Budget Law 59.4
Revenue-Sharing by Area of Origin			
Mineral royalties net of strategic projects	Included May 2015, effective 2016, suspended, reintroduced 2019	60.2.6 60.5	Area of origin Budget Law 60.5
License fees exploration and exploitation	Included May 2015, effective FY2016, suspended, reintroduced 2019	60.2.7 60.6	Area of origin Budget Law 60.6

2. Changing Sharing Rates			2013 Actual	2014 Actual	2016 Actual	2017 (Original)	2017 (Revised)
Budget Law Article	State Budget Revenue Source	Allocation Basis	% State Budget	% State Budget	% State Budget	% State Budget	% State Budget
59.1.1	Domestic VAT	GLDF 4 Criteria Formula	25%	25%	10%	5%	5%
59.1.2	Mining Royalties	Equal per Capita + 10% Premium for Mining Areas	5%	5%	5%	5%	5%
59.1.4	Local Budget Surplus	GLDF 4 Criteria Formula	100%	100%	100%	Suspended	Suspended
59.1.5	Petroleum Royalties	GLDF 4 Criteria Formula			30%	30%	30%
60.2.6	Mining Royalties Net Strategic Projects	Mining Area Origin			30%	10%	Suspended
60.2.7	Mining Exploration Licenses	Mining Area Origin			50%	50%	Suspended
	Base Expenditure Deductions		No	No	No	Yes	Yes
	Sharing ratios for net LDF resources		% share	% share	% share	% share	% share
		Aimag Sub-pool	40%	40%	40%	70%	70%
		Soum/District Sub-pool	60%	60%	60%	30%	30%

FY = fiscal year, GLDF = General Local Development Fund, NGO = nongovernment organization.

Sources: Analysis of the annual Budget Law revisions and data from Ministry of Finance officials.

Table A1.2: Local Development Fund Performance Criteria

Serial No.	Law or Regulation	Articles	Performance Criteria	Indicators	Absolute or Relative Measure	Scoring (maximum score)
FISCAL YEAR 2018: CITIZEN PARTICIPATION FOR FY N BUDGET PRIORITIES						
1	BL Regulation #244	63.1, 12.2.1.a, 12.2.1.c	*Bagh* governors have organized citizen poll to discuss and vote on LDF investment priorities for FY N	*Bagh* governor conducted opinion poll by using Questionnaire Form 8 or organized open discussion or used electronic form by 30 April	R	10
2	Regulation #244	12.2.2		*Bagh* governor clearly stated: location, purpose, scope, etc. of the LDF investment programs and projects when preparing its list for the discussion of bagh meeting	R	8
3	LATUG Regulation #43	23.10, 5.2	*Bagh* governor has organized citizen meeting to discuss and vote on LDF investment priorities for FY N (meeting to be announced two weeks before)	Evidence that *bagh* citizens meeting had organized with valid attendance/quorum (>1 persons from 4 h/h from *soums*, >1 persons from 30 h/h from *aimag soum*) was met, for all *baghs*	R	5
4	Regulation #43	5.7, 5.8, 5.9		LDF investment project proposals from *bagh* meetings actually prioritized based on the "vote" of citizens	A	5
5	Regulation #244	12.2.4	*Bagh* governor has submitted *bagh* meeting proposals to *soum* governor by 30 June FY N-1	Evidence of receipt by *soum* Governor's Office of resolutions from all *baghs* by due date	R	5
BUDGET PREPARATION FOR FY 2017 BUDGET						
6		12.2.5 (12.2.5c)	*Soum* technical working group to develop costed investment proposals based on *bagh* priorities is established and operational	Governor's resolution indicating working group membership	A	5
7	MOF #244			Working group meeting minutes and resolutions showing the group has met more than once and worked to develop project proposals	R	5
8		12.2.5d	Quality and completeness of investment project proposals	Completeness of investment proposals: benefits, costings, recurrent cost estimates; local submissions selected and rejected from original *bagh* list	R	10
9	MOF #43	4.1	Investment proposals consistent with local development policy and planning and PIP priorities	Investment proposals shows clear indication of linkage with local development plans	R	5
10	IBL, MOF #244	63.4/ 12.2.5a–b	Investment proposals reflect *bagh* priorities	Projects in proposed investment program are a subset of those in resolutions from *bagh* meetings and do not include proposals not proposed by *baghs*	A	5

continued on next page

Table A1.2: *Continued*

Serial No.	Law or Regulation	Articles	Performance Criteria	Indicators	Absolute or Relative Measure	Scoring (maximum score)
11	IBL	8.5.4	*Soum hurals* discuss and approve *soum* budget by 20 December FY N-2	*Soum hural* meeting held by due date	A	5
12	LATUG	23.7		*Soum hural* meeting with attendance above quorum	R	10
13	MOF #43	5.10		*Soum hural* meeting minutes indicating LDF investment programs and projects were actually debated and approved	R	8
14	MOF #43	3.3.3, 5.10	Budget documentation clearly indicates list of costed projects and details	Approved budget has clearly specified and costed projects in Attachment 3 of MOF #244	A	8
15	IBL	31.1.6	*Soum* budgets include a procurement plan to implement the approved projects	Procurement plans indicate appropriate procurement methods for each new LDF investment	R	10
	Y2012-264	1.2				
	GR #68					
TRANSPARENCY AND DISCLOSURE FOR FY2016, 2017 BUDGETS						
16	IBL	6.5.2	Actual public attendance at the budget meeting(s)	Budget meeting minutes indicating actual attendance of the public	R	8
17	IBL	6.5.1	*Soum* governor has made budget-related reports public	Budget announcement was clear and accessible to the public	R	10
18	GAL	6.1.2	Glass account is updated regularly according to the law	Evidence that approved budget and allocation and its execution information is entered/updated on due date in glass account website	A	8
BUDGET EXECUTION FOR FY N-2 AND N-1 BUDGETS						
19	IBL	60.3	Proper use of LDF funds	Evidence that LDF is not used for prohibited projects or activities	A	5
20	PPL, MOF #212	47	*Soum* procurement evaluation committees established for each projects that are above threshold	Resolution indicating establishment and membership, compliant with PPL provisions for every tender	A	5
21				All members signed "no conflict of interest" commitment	A	5
22	PPL	21	Tender process is compliant with the laws and regulation	Evidence of tender process is published to the public: e-procurement website and public press	A	8
23		27, 28, 29		Evidence that all contractors awarded are qualified and certified for the particular activity	R	10
24	MOF #43	10.1	Preparation of 6-monthly *soum* LDF implementation report to *aimag* (by 10 July and 1 February)	Copies of LDF implementation reports with recommendations for improvement and evidence of transmission by due dates	R	5

continued on next page

Table A1.2: *Continued*

Serial No.	Law or Regulation	Articles	Performance Criteria	Indicators	Absolute or Relative Measure	Scoring (maximum score)
25	MOF #415	4	LDF projects payments based on the certification of implementation performance	Evidence that payments based on inspection and certification by technical expert	R	10
26	MOF #43	5.11	Approval for budget carry over for investment projects whose implementation overruns the fiscal year	Where there are delays meaning LDF-funded investment implementation overruns into the following fiscal year, evidence that the procedure for approving carryover has been undertaken	A	5
MONITORING AND INSPECTION OF FY N–2 AND N–1 BUDGETS						
27	MOF #43	11.1, 11.2	MIS is regularly and accurately updated	LDF activities planning information has been entered into MIS on due date	A	5
28				LDF-funded projects' implementation, and financing information is entered into MIS is accurate and complete	A	5
29	MOF #43	9.1	Monitoring and inspection of LDF implementation by *hural* inspection	*Hural* inspection committee, citizens, and civil society has conducted the inspection/monitoring on	R	10
30	MOF #43	9.4	The inspection committee together with citizen and civil society shall conduct M&E on the LDF activity result	Adequate parties have taken joint assessment/evaluation on LDF project outcome and results	R	8
SOUM ASSET OWNERSHIP AND MAINTENANCE						
31	MOF #415	4.5.10	Completed LDF investments formally handed over to acceptance committee	Evidence that acceptance committee has established	A	8
32				Acceptance committee undertaken proper inspection for completed LDF investments	R	8
33	LOP, MOF #43	25, 3.4, 8.6	Completed LDF investments registered as *soum* assets	Evidence that *soum* investments duly registered as *soum* property and assigned to the legal entities registration	R	5
					Total	**232**

FY N = fiscal year "n", LDF = Local Development Fund, M&E = monitoring & evaluation, MIS = management information system, MOF = Ministry of Finance, PIP = public investment program, PPL = Public Procurement Law.

Note: *bagh* = rural ward, *soum* = district.

Source: Data from Ministry of Finance. *PIU for Sustainable Livelihood Project – Phase 3*. Ulaanbaatar.

Table A1.3: Bayantal *Soum* (Govisumber *Aimag*) Budget Structure

General

- Human population: 1,240 persons
- Livestock population: 56,000
- *Baghs*: 2
- *Hural*: 15 members

Service Facilities and/or Budget Units

- Health clinic (10 beds)
- Kindergarten with mobile facility for *ger* areas
- Secondary school
- Dormitory (for herders' children)
- Cultural center

N.B. Services also provided to people from neighboring soums

Fiscal Status

Deficit: Receiving MNT258 million in deficit transfer from *aimag*, equivalent to 17.5% of all revenues, in addition to special-purpose transfers (82%) and Local Development Fund (4%).

ORIGINAL AND REVISED BUDGETS, 2017

Expenditure Type	SOUM EXPENDITURES – MNT'000			
	Approved by Parliament	Budget Revision Change (Increase)	Revised Budget	Share of Total Expenditures
Soum hural	39,451.00	5,611.60	45,062.60	3.0%
Soum Governor's Office	202,543.40	8,175.10	210,718.50	14.3%
Soum Bagh governors	21,446.70	3816.6	25,263.30	1.7%
Total expenditure of the *soum* administration	**263,441.10**	**17,603.30**	**281,044.40**	**19.0%**
School No. 4	429,324.90	2,800.00	432,124.90	29.2%
Kindergarten No. 4	158,698.30	3,900.00	162,598.30	11.0%
Cultural center	57,795.50	1,500.00	59,295.50	4.0%
Health center	229,575.70	4,800.00	234,375.70	15.9%
Total delegated social expenditures	**875,394.40**	**13,000.00**	**888,394.40**	**60.1%**
LDF investments, projects, and activities	**263,931.50**	**15,004.60**	**278,936.10**	**18.9%**
Soum development fund expenditures	19,917.70	0.00	19,917.70	1.3%
Livestock protection fund expenditures	9,400.00	0.00	9,400.00	0.6%
Environmental protection fund expenditures	200.00	0.00	200.00	0.0%
Total special fund expenditures	**29,517.70**	**0.00**	**29,517.70**	**2.0%**
TOTAL EXPENDITURE	**1,432,284.70**	**45,607.90**	**1,477,892.60**	**100.0%**

continued on next page

Table A1.3: *Continued*

Revenue Type	SOUM REVENUES – MNT'000			
	Approved by Parliament	Budget Revision Change (Increase)	Revised Budget	Share of total Revenues
Operational revenue	2,000.00	0.00	2,000.00	0.1%
Personal income tax	2,800.00	0.00	2,800.00	0.2%
Firearms excise tax	250.00	0.00	250.00	0.0%
State stamp duty	1,000.00	0.00	1,000.00	0.1%
Waste collection service fee	9,500.00	0.00	9,500.00	0.6%
Total tax revenue of the *soum*	**15,550.00**		**15,550.00**	**1.1%**
Own revenue of special-purpose (SP) transfer entity	1,000.00	0.00	1,000.00	0.1%
Total own revenue of SP transfer entities	**1,000.00**		**1,000.00**	**0.1%**
LDF remaining funding for 2016	203,962.50	0.00	203,962.50	13.8%
2016 wool rebate	0.00	2384.7	2384.7	0.2%
2016 balance (LDF)	0.00	12,619.90	12,619.90	0.9%
LDF 2016 balance	**203,962.50**	**15,004.60**	**218,967.10**	**14.8%**
Financial support from *aimag* center	240,600.50	17,603.30	258,203.80	17.5%
SP transfers from *aimag* budget	874,394.40	13,000.00	887,394.40	60.0%
LDF transfer	59,969.00	0.00	59,969.00	4.1%
Surplus from 2016 base balance	7,290.60	0.00	7,290.60	0.5%
Total transfers from *aimag* **budget**	**1,182,254.50**	**30,603.30**	**1,212,857.80**	**82.1%**
Soum development fund	19,917.70	0.00	19,917.70	1.3%
Livestock protection fund	9,400.00	0.00	9,400.00	0.6%
Environmental protection fund	200.00	0.00	200.00	0.0%
Total other grants	**29,517.70**	**0.00**	**29,517.70**	**2.0%**
TOTAL REVENUE	**1,432,284.70**	**45,607.90**	**1,477,892.60**	**100.0%**

LDF = Local Development Fund.

APPENDIX 2

KEY DONOR PROGRAMS

United Nations Development Programme

(i) With Swiss Agency for Development and Cooperation (SDC) co-funding, supports the Cabinet Secretariat to implement the second phase of the Citizen Representative *Hural* Project. This aims to

    a.   continue capacity support to elected *hural* (elected assembly) members in all *aimags* (provinces) and *soums* (districts) begun in the first phase;

    b.   provide support to the National Academy of Governance to improve its role in subnational government (SNG) support; and

    c.   undertake a review of constitutional and legal reform issues affecting SNGs and local *hurals* (e.g., governor–*hural* accountabilities, SNG service delivery responsibilities, *aimag–soum* division of responsibilities).

(ii) Supports SNG capacities for delivering on Sustainable Development Goals (SDGs) in Ulaanbaatar and Orkhon *aimag*.

(iii) Supports the development of program-based budgeting approaches, especially in health, together with the Asian Development Bank, the National Development Agency, the National Statistics Office, and the Ministry of Finance.

(iv) Supports National Development Agency and National Statistics Office to revise or update Local Development Index data (used, for example, in the allocation of the General Local Development Fund).

(v) Supports assessment of the overall financing implications of the SDGs.

(vi) Supports assessment of SNG use of tax and fee revenues on local natural resource management to promote local biodiversity.

(vii) Supports an assessment of the use of anti-air-pollution financing in Ulaanbaatar.

United Nations Children's Fund

(i) Supports a pilot implemented by the Cabinet Secretariat, National Development Agency, the Ministry of Finance, and sector ministries for improved sector budgeting for health, education, and water, sanitation and hygiene in Ulaanbaatar, Darkhan-Uul, and Bayankhongor *aimags*.

(ii) Supports the Cabinet Secretariat in monitoring SNG governors' performance in spending on education.

World Bank

(i) Supports the Ministry of Finance in implementing the Sustainable Livelihood Project Phase 3 (SLP3), with SDC co-funding. This aims to:

   a. Provide capacity support to all *soums* for better overall governance and public financial management, especially the use of the Local Development Fund (LDF).

   b. Provide capacity support to the Ministry of Finance and *aimags* to play their support role to *soums*.

   c. Introduce a performance-based funding mechanism around the LDF.

(ii) Supports the Cabinet Secretariat and, with SDC co-funding, implements the Mainstreaming Social Accountability in Mongolia Project, which aims to promote greater transparency to and engagement by citizens for services delivered.

Swiss Agency for Development and Cooperation

Aside from several projects noted above, SDC directly funds and supports implementation of:

(i) **Decentralization Support Project.** This project supports the Cabinet Secretariat on:

   a. Overall policy development on decentralization, and more specifically the introduction of a methodology to review SNG functional assignments and to ensure the equalization of SNG financing.

   b. Introduction of a methodology to review and rationalize SNG functional assignments. Initial piloting has been undertaken in the Ministry of Environment, which is now being extended to the Ministry of Construction and Labour. The next step will be to assess the capacities of SNGs to adopt new functions. The Cabinet Secretariat officially endorsed this methodology in a January 2018 circular to all ministries. The Budget Law also included a provision under Article 58 that each ministry should review SNG assignments every 3–5 years.

(ii) **Urban Governance Project.** This project provides support through The Asia Foundation to the Ulaanbaatar municipality to improve service planning and delivery by means of:

   a. A staff capacity development program with a greater focus on staff performance and evaluation.

   b. Piloting a smartphone application to assist Ulaanbaatar Policy and Planning Department to track citizen proposals for the LDF in selected Ulaanbaatar *khoroos* (urban ward), with a view to replicating in other *aimags*.

   c. Piloting a livelihood support council in selected *khoroos*, to assist in targeting social welfare benefits to the neediest.

(iii) **Energy Efficiency Project.** This project provides support through GIZ to build SNG capacities for investment planning and asset management, especially around retrofitting kindergartens, to reduce energy consumption, particularly during winter. After initial piloting in Zavkhan *Aimag*, this is now being tested in Ulaanbaatar, along with the development of a Public Investment Manual for more general use in the city.

(iv) **Support to LOGIN-Asia.** This support has mobilized Kerala Institute of Local Administration to provide training support to Ulaanbaatar and undertaken a review of SLP3 capacity building and prospects for horizontal learning initiatives.

The Asia Foundation

The Asia Foundation has been working in Mongolia since 1993 and has supported a wide range of projects to enhance local government capacity. Past efforts have included efforts to improve local citizen participation, enhance local environmental management by SNGs, improve the legal framework around participation and planning, and improve service delivery in urban centers with a focus in Ulaanbaatar. Ongoing projects include

(i)   Urban Governance Project.

(ii) Waste and Climate Change Project. This project works with the Ministry of Environment and Tourism and the Municipality of Ulaanbaatar to improve data on waste generation, transportation, and management and is improving the policy environment around waste management with a focus on reducing and managing waste. The project is also developing an analysis on which environmentally sound technologies best match the needs of the waste management sector in Mongolia.

(iii) Secondary Cities Project. This project supports Darkhan *Aimag* to develop ArcGIS capacity and improve the use of data for urban planning.[1] Training is being provided to students and government officials. A base map for analysis is being produced that can be used to introduce data relating to a range of urban management challenges.

Mercy Corps

Mercy Corps has a long-standing presence in Mongolia. It has earlier extended support to

- SNG *hurals* and *aimag* governors.
- SNG-CSO partnerships.
- *Hural* oversight through the former President's Office.
- Mongolian Association of Local Authorities.
- Local procurement and A3 training (under the SDC GDP).

Mercy Corps now extends support to:

- local economic development,
- local governance, and
- natural resource management and disaster management.

Open Society Foundation (Mongolia)

- Conducts a biannual survey on SNG transparency in all *aimags* and Ulaanbaatar.
- Supports 20 nongovernment organizations in a few aimags to monitor the transparency of public spending and implementing the Glass Account Law and to hold public hearings around the results.

---

[1]   ArcGIS is a geographic information system for working with maps and geographic information maintained by the Environmental Systems Research Institute.

www.ingramcontent.com/pod-product-compliance
Lightning Source LLC
Chambersburg PA
CBHW050048220326
41599CB00045B/7332